Lectio Divina
Assimilating the Holy Word in Seminary Formation

Edited by
James Keating

Institute for Priestly Formation
IPF Publications

CONTRIBUTORS

Father Llane B. Briese, STL, STD, is Dean of Pastoral Formation, Associate Professor of Sacred Scripture, and Director of Liturgy at St. Vincent dePaul Regional Seminary in Boynton Beach, Florida.

Ximena DeBroeck, STL, PhD, is Seminary Professor and former Administrator of Pastoral Formation at Mount St. Mary's Seminary in Emmitsburg, Maryland.

Stephen Fahrig, STL, STD, is Associate Professor of Biblical Theology at Kenrick-Glennon Seminary in St. Louis, Missouri.

Deacon James Keating, PhD, is General Editor of IPF Publications at the Institute for Priestly Formation in Omaha, Nebraska and Professor of Spiritual Theology at Kenrick-Glennon Seminary in St. Louis, Missouri.

Father Mark O'Keefe, O.S.B., STL, STD, is Professor of Moral Theology at Saint Meinrad Seminary and School of Theology in St. Meinrad, Indiana.

William M. Wright IV, PhD, is Professor of Catholic Studies and Theology at Duquesne University in Pittsburgh, Pennsylvania.

INSTITUTE FOR PRIESTLY FORMATION
IPF Publications
11626 Nicholas Street
Omaha, Nebraska 68154
www.IPFPublications.com

Copyright © July 18, 2023 by
Institute for Priestly Formation, Inc.

All Rights Reserved. No part of this book may be reproduced, stored in a retrieval system, or transmitted by any
means, electronic, mechanical, photocopying, recording, or
otherwise, without the written permission of the Institute for
Priestly Formation.

Printed in the United States of America
ISBN-13: 979-8-9859345-5-7

Scripture texts in this work are taken from the New American
Bible, revised edition © 2010, 1991, 1986, 1970 Confrater-
nity of Christian Doctrine, Washington, D.C. and are used by
permission of the copyright owner. All Rights Reserved. No
part of the New American Bible may be reproduced in any
form without permission in writing from the copyright owner.

Cover design by Timothy D. Boatright

INSTITUTE *for* PRIESTLY FORMATION

MISSION STATEMENT

In collaboration with Catholic seminaries and dioceses, we form seminarians, priests, and bishops in holiness and accompany them in their ongoing spiritual growth, so they can more effectively lead others to Christ.

INSTITUTE FOR PRIESTLY FORMATION
11626 Nicholas Street
Omaha, Nebraska 68154
www.priestlyformation.org
ipf@priestlyformation.org

TABLE OF CONTENTS

INTRODUCTION

The *Program of Priestly Formation* promotes the habit of *lectio divina* as a substantive way for seminarians to hear God's communication.[1] To embrace the celibate vocation, a priest defines himself as eager to deepen his friendship with the Most Holy Trinity. Without such friendship, the celibate will rest his heart in work or vacations or even illicit relations or habits. Founding one's love upon a prayerful vulnerability to the living Word, God communicating Himself through Holy Scripture, assures a man of authentic rest, authentic love. Such vulnerability, a life of contemplative encounter with God through His presence in the Word, bears much fruit in personal peace and creativity, dynamic ministry and preaching, and faithful teaching of parishioners in the ways of prayer. The Church holds out Scripture to the seminarian not simply as a "course of studies" but as a source to quench his thirst for intimacy with God. In so doing, the Church demands that seminarians enter profoundly into the contemplation of the person of Jesus Christ, thus assuming the priestly identity.[2]

In this book, several Scripture scholars and a veteran seminary professor take the reader into the essence of Scripture as living, as an encounter with a Divine Person, as a way of prayer. Such a journey is not sentimental emotivism, however,

1

but simply the fruit of faith-filled intellects pondering, in discipline, the One whom their heart seeks. As Pope Emeritus Benedict XVI notes in *Verbum Domini,*

> The study of Scripture ought to lead to an increased awareness of the mystery of divine revelation and foster an attitude of prayerful response to the Lord who speaks. Conversely, an authentic life of prayer cannot fail to nurture in the candidate's heart a desire for greater knowledge of the God who has revealed himself in his word as infinite love. Hence, great care should be taken to ensure that seminarians always cultivate this *reciprocity between study and prayer* in their lives. This end will be served if candidates are introduced to the study of Scripture through methods which favour [*sic*] this integral approach.[3]

I hope that both seminary faculty and seminarians will take the time to reflect upon the research shared within these pages. Ours is an age where it is urgent to promote a faith-imbued study of the Scriptures as so much of the world has turned away from both faith and reason and now exists bereft upon a sea of superficiality, ideology, and distraction. May the next generation of priests lead us back to sanity and sanctity.

Deacon James Keating, PhD
General Editor of IPF Publications
Professor of Spiritual Theology
Kenrick Glennon Seminary, St Louis, Missouri

NOTES

1.   United States Conference of Catholic Bishops (USCCB), *Program of Priestly Formation*, 6th ed. (Washington, DC: USCCB, 2022), sec. 123, 229, 249, 254.

2.   Congregation for the Clergy, *Ratio Fundamentalis Institutionis Sacerdotalis* (2016), sec. 68.

3.   Benedict XVI, *Verbum Domini* (2010), sec. 82, emphasis in original.

LECTIO DIVINA AND THE POWERFUL PRESENCE OF GOD'S WORD: INSIGHTS FROM THE VINE AND THE BRANCHES (JOHN 15:1–8)

WILLIAM M. WRIGHT IV

The 2016 *Ratio Fundamentalis Institutionis Sacerdotalis: The Gift of the Priestly Vocation* commends to candidates for Holy Orders the traditional practice of praying with Scripture known as *lectio divina*.[1] The *Ratio* places its discussion of *lectio divina* in a larger section on the spiritual formation of candidates for ordained ministry. The goal of spiritual formation, as the *Ratio* puts it, is "nourishing and sustaining communion with God and with our brothers and sisters in the friendship of Jesus the Good Shepherd."[2] By so identifying the goal of spiritual formation, the *Ratio* positions the various practices discussed in this section as means that aim at realizing this goal.[3] In other words, the *Ratio* invites us to see *lectio divina* as a spiritual practice that is ordered to fostering communion with God and with others in God. It is a way of reading Scripture that is both personal and transformative.

The *Ratio* specifically discusses *lectio divina* in a section that concerns the Scriptures and the Word of God. Here, the *Ratio* talks about the Word of God in terms that likewise accent its personal and transformative aspects. For instance, the *Ratio* introduces this section with Jerome's famous statement from the Prologue of his commentary on Isaiah: "Ignorance of the Scriptures is ignorance of Christ."[4] This opening statement so presents the Scriptures as a means by which readers can know the person of Jesus Christ. From there, the *Ratio* states, "a relationship with the Word of God holds a preeminent place in the process of spiritual growth."[5] Here, the *Ratio* not only identifies the Word of God as a reality with which people can have a relationship, but this relationship with the Word of God is transformative—it can facilitate and nurture spiritual growth. Referencing Origen, the *Ratio* also teaches, "Before it is ever preached, the Word must be welcomed in the depth of the heart."[6] This language recalls Luke's version of the Parable of the Sower (Luke 8:4–8, 11–15), which so interprets the response of the good soil to the seed that is God's Word: "they are the ones who, when they have heard the word, embrace it with a generous and good heart, and bear fruit through perseverance" (Lk 8:15).[7] The *Ratio* thus presents the Word of God as a reality that people can take in and that causes growth and transformation in them.

This understanding of Scripture as mediating the presence and power of the Word of God is explored at length in *Encountering the Living God in Scripture: Theological and Philosophical Principles for Interpretation* (which I co-authored with Father Francis Martin). In this book, Martin and I document how biblical witnesses from both testaments connect the Word of God with causal power and modes of presence.[8] As to the first, the Scriptures teach that God can produce a divinely caused effect through His Word either directly or as mediated through inspired human discourse.[9] As to the second, Christian theological thinking about the Word of God takes its cue from the New Testament teaching that the Word of God is the Divine Person who becomes human in Jesus of Nazareth.[10] Inspired human discourse, including Scripture, is a Spirit-touched means by which the Word of God becomes present in people through their hearing or reading.[11] We then provide an account of those theological and philosophical principles that help us grasp the intelligibility of this belief.

Building upon the account given in *Encountering the Living God in Scripture*, I wish to explore in this essay the personal and transformative aspects of the Word of God given in Scripture, aspects that are ingredient to *lectio divina*, by considering them in light of Jesus's teaching about the vine and the branches in John 15:1–8. This section of John's Gospel befits this topic for it not only speaks of the Word of God as a reality that indwells Jesus's disciples (15:7) but the imagery of the vine and bearing fruit also squares with the *Ratio Fundamentalis*'s use of organic language for Scripture as fostering spiritual growth and communion. These Johannine texts can help us acquire a deeper understanding of the presence and power of the Word of God, whom readers can encounter through the "prayerful reading" of Scripture that is *lectio divina*.[12]

The Vine, the Branches, and the Presence of God's Word

Jesus begins His use of the vine image by first identifying Himself as "the true vine" (Jn 15:1), and He later refers to His disciples as "the branches" (Jn 15:5). Throughout this section, Jesus repeatedly tells His disciples to "remain" [Greek: *menō*] in Him as branches on the vine (Jn 15:4–5, 7, 9). This

Greek word *menō*, usually translated as "remain" or "abide," is a technical term in the Johannine writings, and it often bears a special theological meaning.[13] Important for our purposes is John's use of the verb *menō* (often accompanied by the Greek preposition *en* "in") to express spiritual communion or the union of divine life.[14] For instance, Jesus uses this verbal expression to articulate the union of life between Him and the Father. In the Farewell Discourse, Jesus asks His disciples, "Do you not believe that I am in the Father and the Father is in me" (Jn 14:10)? He immediately develops this statement by declaring that the Father "remains in" Him and "does his works" (14:10). For His part, Jesus says that He "remains in" the Father's "love" (Jn 15:10). This use of *menō* to articulate the union of life between the Father and Son accords with Jesus's prayer of communion in John 17 where He speaks of Himself and the Father as being "one" (Jn 17:11, 21, 23) or as being "in" each other (Jn 17:21, 23).[15]

In this section on the vine and the branches, Jesus uses this language of remaining to designate the spiritual communion, the mystical union of life, that He will share with His disciples through the Holy Spirit.[16] The image of the vine is an organic image, and the emphasis in 15:1–8 is on the flow of life from the vine into the branches. Even before identifying His disciples as the branches in this section, Jesus tells His disciples, "Remain in me, as I remain in you" (Jn 15:4). The disciples' communion with Jesus—their remaining in Him and He in them—is that which enables the disciples to bear fruit. He continues, "Just as a branch cannot bear fruit on its own unless it remains on the vine, so neither can you unless you remain in me" (Jn 15:4).[17]

Significant for our purposes is a shift that occurs in John 15:7. Here, Jesus declares, "If you remain in me and my words remain in you, ask for whatever you want, and it will be done for you" (Jn 15:7). Previously, Jesus spoke of *Himself* as remaining in His disciples, and His disciples as remaining in Him.[18] Now He shifts to speak of His *words* as remaining in the disciples. Both Jesus Himself and His words are said to "remain in" His disciples and, so, constitute this communion of life.

Jesus's statement in John 15:7 recalls His previous statement in 8:31–32. Here, Jesus tells a group of fledgling believers, "If you remain in my word, you will truly be my disciples, and you will know the truth, and the truth will set you free." In 15:7, Jesus's words "remain in" the disciples, and in 8:31, these beginning believers are invited to "remain in [Jesus's] word." Both Jesus Himself and His words are said to "remain in" His disciples, and His disciples are instructed to "remain in" both Jesus Himself and His words.[19] Jesus and His words are, to use the observation of Raymond Brown, "virtually interchangeable, for he is incarnate revelation (the Word)."[20]

The interchangeability between Jesus's person and His Word merits further unpacking. The Prologue of the Gospel identifies Jesus as the divine Word of God.[21] Not only does the Word (or Son) exist with God (the Father) apart from creation, but He is the only one who has ever "seen the Father" (6:46). Since only Jesus, the Incarnate Word, has this divine relationship with the Father, only He can reveal God as Father and Himself as the Son in a unique, unparalleled, and unsurpassable way.[22] Everything about Jesus, as the Son and Word, is constituted by His relationship with the Father: all that Jesus says,[23] does,[24] and is[25] is from the Father. Indeed, "Jesus' whole life—his person, words, and deeds—is a revelation of the Father, of himself as the Son, and of the infinite love between them."[26]

Throughout the Gospel, Jesus also speaks of His revelatory Word in quasi-substantive terms as a kind of reality that can be present in people and act in them. In 15:7, as we have seen, Jesus says that His words can "remain in" His disciples. Earlier in the Gospel, when defending Himself against His opponents' charges, Jesus tells His opponents who do not believe in Him, "the Father who sent me has testified on my behalf . . . and *you do not have his word remaining in you*, because you do not believe in the one whom he has sent (Jn 5:37–38).[27] Since Jesus is Himself the Father's Word and He says and does only what the Father gives Him, Jesus's Word is the Father's Word. The refusal of Jesus's opponents to receive His Word in faith evidences that the Father's Word is not present in them. Put differently, to believe in Jesus is to receive the revelation that He not only speaks but that He Himself is. Faith is a way by which the reality of the Word of God comes to dwell within a person.[28]

Other texts from the Johannine corpus similarly present Jesus's Word as a reality that indwells believers. In 1 John 2:14, the author states, "I write to you, young men, because you are strong and the word of God remains in you." Conversely, those who do not profess orthodox faith do not have the Word of God in them. The author writes, "If we say, 'We have not sinned,' we make him a liar, and his word is not in us" (1 Jn 1:10). Other expressions in 1 John, such as "the anointing" (2:20) and the "seed" (3:9), likewise speak to the Spirit-activated presence of God's Word or revelation in believers.[29] The Word of Jesus is something that can be present in or absent from people, and the Word's indwelling presence or absence is correlated with a person's faith or unbelief in Jesus.

Such statements from the Johannine writings evidence a profound relationship between Jesus and His Word. This relationship between Jesus's self and His Word is comparable to forms of biblical thinking about a person's name.[30] Throughout the Scriptures, a person's name was a verbalization of a person's identity or being. As Eichrodt writes, "the name is regarded as to such an extent an expression of the individual character of its owner that it can, in fact, stand for him, become a concept interchangeable with him."[31] Comparably, we might think of Jesus's Word as a kind of verbalization of Jesus's self. Hence, John's Gospel can speak of both Jesus and His Word as remaining in disciples, and it can speak of the disciples as remaining in both Jesus and His Word. To receive Jesus's revelatory Word in faith is to receive Him. Through faith, the Word of God comes to indwell a person and communicates a share in His divine life.

When we bring these teachings from John's Gospel to bear on *lectio divina*, we are given much insight into the personal and relational dimensions of this faith-filled way of reading Scripture. To begin with, the Johannine writings remind us that when we speak of the Word of God, we are speaking of a "who" more than a "what." John's Gospel teaches that the Word of God is a name for God the Son, that is, the second person of the Trinity.[32] And so, when we take the *Ratio's* statement, "a relationship with the Word of God holds a preeminent place in the process of spiritual growth" in light of John's Gospel, we can understand the mention of the Word of God here as referring to Christ.[33] To say, therefore, that the Scriptures mediate the Word of God is to say that they mediate the reality of the same Divine Person who became incarnate in Jesus Christ. The encounter with the Word of God that Scripture brings about for its readers is an encounter with the person of Jesus Christ.

The *Ratio* also states that "the Word must be welcomed in the depth of the heart."[34] The Johannine writings speak of the Word of God as a reality that can be taken in by people. This happens in the case of those who respond to Jesus and His revelation in faith and discipleship. As believers take in the Word of Jesus, the same Word comes to indwell believers. Those who believe in Jesus thus enter into communion with Him and, through Him, with the Father. Hence, Jesus and His Word remain in believers; and believers, in turn, remain in Jesus and His Word.

These Johannine teachings speak to the necessity of reading the Scriptures in faith. If people, especially candidates for ordination, are to have "a relationship with the Word of God" and if "the Word of God must be welcomed in the depth of the heart," then a living faith on the part of readers is a necessity.[35] It is through faith that the Word of God comes to indwell people—and conversely, the Word does not indwell those who do not believe.[36] As Benedict XVI writes in *Verbum Domini*, "authentic biblical hermeneutics can only be had within the faith of the Church."[37] He later quotes Bonaventure, commenting on faith as a necessity for rightly understanding the Scriptures: "It is impossible for anyone to attain to knowledge of that truth unless he first have infused faith in Christ, which is the lamp, the gate, and the foundation of all Scripture."[38]

Pope Francis has likewise spoken about the importance of reading the Bible with the Church's faith, not simply in *lectio divina* but also in Catholic biblical scholarship as such.[39] In a 2014 address to the Italian Biblical Association, Francis sets forth a reciprocity between the Church's faith and the Word of God. Francis observes that the Church's faith is today "assailed . . . by contrasting cultural stimuli," and in order for "the faith to respond, to avoid being suffocated, it must be constantly nourished by the Word of God."[40] He goes on to teach that in order for biblical exegetes to help the faithful discern the Word of God in Scripture, the exegetes themselves must first be related to the Word of God by faith. He states, "it is of course necessary that the exegete himself be able to perceive in the text the divine Word—and this is possible only if his spiritual life is fervent, rich in dialogue with the Lord; otherwise exegetical research is incomplete, losing sight of its main objective."[41] The Pope even commends the importance of the exegete's faith as being as much of an interpretive priority as scholarly expertise: "In addition to academic competence, what is required of the Catholic exegete first and foremost is faith, received and shared with the body of believing people."[42] There is, therefore, a reciprocity between the Word of God and the Church's faith. The Church's faith allows the reader to discern the Word of God in Scripture; and the Word of God, in turn, nourishes and deepens the faith of believers who encounter Him in Scripture.

The Vine, the Branches, and the Power of God's Word

As the vine is the source of life for its branches, so Jesus teaches that His disciples must remain in spiritual communion with Him. In John 15:1–8, the flow of life from the vine into the branches also enables the branches to produce fruit. Jesus underscores this point: "Whoever remains in me and I in him will bear much fruit, because without me you can do nothing" (Jn 15:5). As branches are able to produce fruit only because they are connected to the vine as their source of life, so too are the disciples able to produce fruit only because of their spiritual communion with Jesus. Put differently, the vine has causal power vis-à-vis the branches.

The deep connection in the Johannine writings between Jesus's person and His Word would suggest that Jesus's Word, in addition to being a form of His presence, can also have a causal effect in the disciples. That is, the indwelling Word of God has the power to change believers from within.

The causal power of Jesus's Word comes to light through certain connections it has with the Father's actions described in 15:1–8. After introducing himself as "the true vine" (15:1), Jesus identifies His Father as the "vine grower" (15:1). He then names two actions that the Father does with respect to the branches: first, "he takes away every branch in me that does not bear fruit" (15:2); second, "every one that does he prunes [Greek: *kathairei*] so that it bears more fruit" (15:2). The Father's actions are directed to the production of fruit. As the vine grower, the Father removes branches that do not bear fruit, and He also prunes healthy branches so that they can produce even more fruit. The Father, thus, works in Jesus's disciples to enable them to grow spiritually.

Jesus then says that His Word produces this same divinely caused effect in the disciples, and to make this claim, He uses the same language as He did to talk about the Father's action as the Vine Grower. He tells His disciples, "You are already pruned [Greek: *katharoi*] because of the word that I have spoken to you" (15:3). Jesus here identifies the effects that His

Word produces in His disciples with the effects that His Father produces in the branches: that is, both the Father and Jesus's Word render the branches as "pruned." The goal of such pruning is to enable the disciples to produce more fruit. In other words, when taken in by His disciples in faith, Jesus's Word can transform them from within. Jesus's Word not only mediates His presence but also divine power.

The context of John 15 suggests that the fruits that the Father seeks from the branches are works of love.[43] Immediately after teaching about the vine and the branches (15:1–8), Jesus gives His disciples the love command (15:9–17), and there are several verbal and thematic connections between these two sections.

We have seen that Jesus teaches His disciples to remain in union with Him as branches remain connected to the vine (15:4–5). The way in which the disciples remain in communion with Him (i.e., remain attached to the vine) is through their obedience: "If you keep my commandments, you will remain in my love, just as I have kept my Father's commandments and remain in his love" (15:10). The commandment that Jesus gives to His disciples to obey is the love command: "love one another as I love you" (15:12). It is through their love (and obedience) that disciples preserve their spiritual communion with Jesus.

As previously discussed, Jesus teaches that the Father removes from the vine those branches that do not produce fruit. Taken in light of 15:10, these branches/disciples are those who do not obey Jesus's love command. That is, they do not love and obey, and hence, they are not in communion with Jesus. Conversely, those branches that both remain on the vine and produce fruit are the disciples who do obey Jesus's love command. Hence, the fruit that these disciples produce by virtue of their communion with Jesus is love. Moreover, the Father continues to prune and nurture these branches so that they can "[bear] more fruit" (15:2). The loving conduct of Jesus's disciples, which their communion with the indwelling Word of God enables them to produce, is the fruit cultivated by the Father. As Jesus later teaches in the context of the love command, "I . . . chose you and [I] appointed you to go and bear fruit that will remain" (15:16).

This relationship between remaining in communion with God and doing works of love likewise appears in 1 John.[44] In his opening exposition, the author writes, "whoever claims to abide in him ought to live [just] as he lived" (2:6).[45] The reality of the believer's spiritual communion with God (i.e., remaining in Him) manifests itself in the Godly conduct of that believer. Thus, as the author establishes that "God is light, and in him there is no darkness at all" (1:5), he can later state, "Whoever loves his brother remains in the light" (2:10). On several occasions, the author of 1 John speaks of Jesus's love command.[46] Similar to the Fourth Gospel, believers' loving practice flows from and manifests their spiritual communion with God: "Those who keep his commandments remain in him, and he in them" (3:24). As Spicq puts it, in 1 John, "To love—both God and one's brothers—presupposes that we are begotten by God and that God's seed lives in us; we manifest his love, live it, and act because of it."[47]

In these Johannine texts, we see that believers are brought into a communion of life with Jesus, the Word of God. The Word of God comes to indwell believers through faith. The indwelling Word constitutes the source of vital power that flows into the disciples and enables them to bear the fruit that is loving conduct. The loving conduct and obedience of believers not only preserves their communion with the indwelling Word, but the power of the indwelling Word (as well as the Father's action in believers) enables believers to love more intensely and deeply. In short, the indwelling Word is not only a mode of God's presence in believers but a source of his life-transforming power.

The *Ratio* similarly uses organic language to talk about the power of the Word of God to effect change in people's lives. The *Ratio* commends *lectio divina* because "a relationship with the Word of God holds a preeminent place in the process of spiritual growth."[48] In a footnote attached to this statement, the *Ratio* cites Benedict XVI, who likewise speaks of *lectio divina* as a relational practice ordered to growth: "Those aspiring to the ministerial priesthood are called to a profound personal relationship with God's word, particularly in *lectio divina*, so that this relationship will in turn nurture their vocation."[49] The *Ratio* speaks of the Word of God as involved in the process of "spiritual growth," and Benedict XVI similarly speaks of a candidate's relationship with the Word as able to "nurture" a priestly vocation. When discussing spiritual formation (of which *lectio divina* is a constituent practice), the *Ratio* uses the organic language of "nourishing and sustaining communion with God."[50] These references all speak of the Word of God, whom believers can encounter through Scripture, as causing growth and sustaining life. In short, the Word of God can work transformation in people who receive it in faith.

The previously examined Johannine texts present the indwelling Word of God as a source of vital, life-transforming power. The vine is what gives life to the branches and enables them to produce, and so Jesus is the source of spiritual life and power for His disciples. Accordingly, Jesus teaches that His disciples must absolutely remain in communion with Him if they are to have spiritual life and produce fruit: "As a branch cannot bear fruit on its own unless it remains on the vine, so neither can you unless you remain in me" (15:4).[51] Both the Father and the indwelling Word work within those disciples in communion so that they can produce more fruit (i.e., to love more deeply and intensely). For their part, believers welcome the Word of God into themselves through faith, and this relationship with the Word must grow. As Peter had to yield to Jesus and allow Jesus to wash his feet (John 13:8–9), so must believers yield to the work of the Word and of the Father to prune them.[52]

The Word of God, whom we encounter in Scripture, take in by faith, and so enter into communion with, works to transform our lives. The fruit of this transformative relationship with the indwelling Word is love. The goal of *lectio divina*, therefore, is to nurture this vital relationship with the Word of God and allow Him to transform one's life to become more faithful and loving. The *Ratio* gets at this point when it states that the goal of spiritual formation (which *lectio divina* seeks to help realize) is "communion with God *and with our brothers and sisters*."[53] The more one is brought into communion with the Word and yields to His action then the more intensely will that communion issue forth in love.

The famous parsing of *lectio divina* in four steps was made by the monk Guigo II of Chartreuse in his work *The Ladder of Monks*.[54] He identifies the four steps as reading, meditation, prayer, and contemplation.[55] Some have highlighted a place for action that is implied in this vision. Commenting on the prayerful reading of Scripture in the Franciscan tradition, Magrassi writes the following about Francis of Assisi and the Scriptures: "he was firmly convinced that it is useless to know the sacred verses if this does not lead to action."[56] Benedict XVI makes a similar claim in *Verbum Domini*. He writes, "We do well also to remember that the process of *lectio divina* is not concluded until it arrives at action (*actio*), which moves the believer to make his or her life a gift for others in charity."[57] We are, thus, reminded that the goal of reading the Bible in faith is the intellectual, moral, and spiritual transformation of human beings. The source that works this transformation of life in us is the Word of God, whom we can encounter and take in through the faith-filled prayed reading of Scripture.

Conclusion

The 2016 *Ratio Fundamentalis* prescribes *lectio divina* as an important component for the spiritual formation of candidates for ordained ministry. These reflections on John's Gospel give us further insight into why the prayerful reading of Scripture has such an important role. Jesus is Himself the Word of God, and as we see in John's Gospel, Jesus's own words are closely connected to His person. When people receive Jesus in faith, the Word of God that Jesus speaks, and which He Himself is, comes to indwell believers. Believers can encounter this same Word of God through the prayerful reading of Scripture that is *lectio divina*. The indwelling Word of God also has causal power to transform the lives of believers as they yield to His action and that of His Father within us. The power of the Word aims to transform our lives so that they might bear more fruits which are works of love, and we yield to the divine work in us through receptive, obedient faith.

In a 2021 audience, Pope Francis aptly brings together these topics of the indwelling Word of God, its life-changing power, and the prayerful reading of Scripture:

> Through prayer, the Word of God comes to abide in us and we abide in it. The Word inspires good intentions and sustains action; it gives us strength and serenity, and even when it challenges us, it gives us peace. On "bad" and confusing days, it guarantees to the heart a core of confidence and of love that protects it from the attacks of the evil one.[58]

Seen in light of these Johannine teachings, we can appreciate more the importance of *lectio divina* as a spiritual practice. It is a way by which believers today can encounter the presence and transformative power of the Word of God Himself. When we open ourselves to Him by reading Scripture with a receptive, yielding faith, we open ourselves to His life-giving and life-changing power. And so, in the words of Pope Francis, "let us grow passionate about sacred scripture, let us be willing to dig deep within the word that reveals God's newness and leads us tirelessly to love others."[59]

NOTES

1. Congregation for the Clergy, *Ratio Fundamentalis Institutionis Sacerdotalis* (2016), sec. 103.

2. Ibid., sec. 101.

3. Along with *lectio divina*, the *Ratio* lists a number of practices under spiritual formation: silent prayer (sec. 102), the Eucharist (sec. 104), the Liturgy of the Hours (sec. 105), the Sacrament of Confession and the daily examination of conscience (sec. 106), spiritual direction (sec. 107), annual retreats (sec. 108), development of the evangelical counsels as appropriate to the particular clerical state (sec. 109–111), devotion to the Blessed Virgin Mary, Saint Joseph, and other saints (sec. 112), study of the Church Fathers (sec. 113), various forms of piety (sec. 114), and the development of virtues appropriate to pastoral ministry (sec. 115).

4. *Ratio*, sec. 103, citing (p. 45 n.155) from Jerome, *Commentarii in Isaiam*, Prologus: *Corpus Christianorum Series Latina* 73.1, italics removed.

5. *Ratio*, sec. 103.

6. Ibid. While it does not specify the exact part of the sermon, the *Ratio* references Origen, *Homilia in Lucam* 32.2 (*Patrologia Graeca* 13:1884).

7. On the Parable of the Sower and its relation to the spiritual reading of Scripture, see William M. Wright IV and Francis Martin, *Encountering the Living God in Scripture: Theological and Philosophical Principles for Interpretation* (Grand Rapids: Baker Academic, 2019), 232–236.

8. Wright and Martin, *Encountering*, 13–36. We discuss (pp. 3–5) *lectio divina* as a hallmark example of this understanding of Scripture as mediating the power and presence of God's Word.

9. Ibid., 37–99.

10. Ibid., 24. See also John 1:1–3, 14; Revelation 19:13.

11. Ibid., 79–99, esp. 85–99.

12. Used on occasion in this essay, the description of *lectio divina* as "prayerful reading" is taken from Jean LeClercq, OSB, *The Love for Learning and the Desire for God: A Study of Monastic Culture*, trans. Catherine Misrahi (New York: Fordham University Press, 1982 [1957]), 73.

13. Other examples of *menō* as denoting the spiritual union of life (or believers' participating in divine life) appear in the Johannine Letters: see 1 John 2:6, 10, 14, 24, 27–28; 3:5, 14, 15, 17, 24; 4:12–13, 15–16; 2 John 2, 9. For discussion, see Raymond E. Brown, SS, *The Gospel according to John*, 2 vols., Anchor Bible 29–29A (New York: Doubleday, 1966–1970), 1.510–512; Craig R. Koester, *The Word of Life: A Theology of John's Gospel* (Grand Rapids: Eerdmans, 2008), 195–196; Ceslaus Spicq, *Agape in the New Testament: Volume 3: Agape in the Gospels, Epistles, and Apocalypse of St. John*, trans. Sister Marie Aquinas McNamara, OP and Sister Mary Honoria Richter, OP (St. Louis: Herder Book Co., 1966; repr. Eugene: Wipf &

Stock, 2006), 36–39; Marianne Meye Thompson, *John*, New Testament Library (Louisville: Westminster John Knox, 2015), 324–325. On this language in 1 John, see Edward Malatesta, SJ, *Interiority and Covenant: A Study of [einai en] and [menein en] in the First Letter of Saint John*, Analecta Biblica 69 (Rome: Biblical Institute Press, 1978).

14.   Spicq (*Agape in the New Testament*, 38) puts it succinctly: "To abide in Christ is to be in vital, mutual, indefectible union with him."

15.   Similarly, the Holy Spirit descends upon Jesus at His Baptism and "remains" on Him (Jn 1:33). Jesus later tells His disciples that the same Holy Spirit, the Paraclete, "remains with you, and will be in you" (Jn 14:17).

16.   See John 15:4–7, 9–10.

17.   See also John 15:5.

18.   See John 15:4.

19.   See John 8:31; 15:4, 7.

20.   Brown, *Gospel according to John*, 2.662.

21.   See John 1:1–3, 14, 17.

22.   See John 1:18.

23.   See John 8:38, 40; 18:37.

24.   See John 5:19; 10:37–38; 14:11.

25.   See John 5:26.

26.   Francis Martin and William M. Wright IV, *The Gospel of John*, Catholic Commentary on Sacred Scripture (Grand Rapids: Baker Academic, 2015), 24.

27.   Emphasis added. See also John 8:37.

28.   A similar picture emerges from the Pauline writings (e.g., Romans 1:16; 10:15–17; 1 Corinthians 1:18–24; 1 Thessalonians 2:13); see the discussion in Wright and Martin, *Encountering*, 61–73.

29.   See Ignace de la Potterie, SJ, "Anointing of the Christian by Faith," in Ignace de la Potterie, SJ and Stanislaus Lyonnet, SJ, *The Christian Lives by the Spirit*, trans. John Morriss (Staten Island: Alba House, 1971), 79–135; repr. from *Biblica* 40 (1959): 12–69. See also 1 John 2:24, 4:15.

30.   Walther Eichrodt, *Theology of the Old Testament*, 2 vols., trans J. A. Baker (Philadelphia: The Westminster Press, 1967), 2.40–45.

31.   Ibid., *Theology of the Old Testament*, 2.40, italics removed.

32.   See John 1:1–4, 14, 18.

33.   *Ratio Fundamentalis*, sec. 103.

34.   Ibid., sec. 103.

35.   Ibid.

36.   See John 5:38.

37.   Benedict XVI, *Verbum Domini* (2010), sec. 29.

38.   Bonaventure, *Breviloquium*, Prol.; cited in Benedict XVI, *Verbum Domini*, sec. 29.

39.   Pope Francis explicitly discusses *lectio divina* in his General Audience of 27 January 2021. Text available at https://www.vatican.va/content/

francesco/en/audiences/2021/documents/papa-francesco_20210127_udi-enza-generale.html. The Pope's remarks on the need to integrate faith and academic study of Scripture are of a piece with the *Ratio Fundamentalis* as well as Benedict XVI's teachings in *Verbum Domini*. The *Ratio* also speaks of the need for such "prayerful reading" to be integrated with the academic study of Scripture that forms part of the seminary curriculum. The text reads, "A profound daily meditation, practiced with fidelity and diligence, in which study and prayer come together in a reciprocal fruitfulness, will ensure an integral approach to both the Old and New Testaments" (*Ratio Fundamentalis*, sec. 103). Here too, the *Ratio* follows the teachings of Benedict XVI in *Verbum Domini*. In *Verbum Domini* section 82, Benedict similarly commends the need to integrate "biblical studies and scriptural prayer" (sec. 82, italics removed). He envisions a situation wherein biblical studies enhance one's grasp of divine revelation and open up into a response of prayer and wish to know the God who reveals more deeply. Benedict concludes this section by writing, "This end will be served if candidates are introduced to the study of Scripture through methods which favor this integral approach" (sec. 82). Benedict also realizes that not all approaches to Scripture and practitioners of biblical studies are amenable to integrating academic learning and the practice of faith. Nevertheless, with this last statement, Benedict implies his wish that biblical studies taught in seminaries would so be open to this "integral approach" that integrates "study and prayer" (sec. 82). This commendation coheres with Benedict's strong exhortation, articulated in *Verbum Domini* and elsewhere, for a more robust integration of exegesis, theology, faith, and philosophy.

40. Francis, "Address of Pope Francis to the Italian Biblical Association," 12 September 2014, https://www.vatican.va/content/francesco/en/speeches/2014/september/documents/papa-francesco_20140912_associazione-biblica-italiana.html (accessed January 28, 2022).

41. Ibid.

42. Ibid.

43. So, too, Gail R. O'Day, *The Gospel of John*, The New Interpreter's Bible IX (Nashville: Abingdon, 1995), 757–758; D. Moody Smith, *The Theology of the Gospel of John* (New York: Cambridge University Press, 1995), 147; Koester, *Word of Life*, 195–196.

44. In addition to the cases mentioned below, see 1 John 2:10, 17; 3:6, 14–15, 17; 4:7–12, 16.

45. The word translated here as "live" is the Greek verb *peripateō* which literally means "to walk around." It reflects the Hebrew use of the verb *hālak* ("to walk") to denote moral living.

46. See 1 John 2:7; 3:11, 23; 4:7, 11.

47. Spicq, *Agape*, 105.

48. *Ratio Fundamentalis*, sec. 103.

49. *Verbum Domini*, sec. 82; referenced in *Ratio Fundamentalis*, sec. 156.

50.   *Ratio Fundamentalis*, sec. 101.

51.   Put differently, unless one remains in spiritual communion with Jesus through sanctifying grace and nurtures this vital relationship with Him through prayer, one should not expect much to come of one's endeavors in the spiritual life: "apart from me, you cannot do anything" (15:5).

52.   The footwashing is a prophetic symbol of the Cross, (i.e., Jesus's self-emptying act of love for the benefit of others). When Jesus tells Peter, "Unless I wash you, you will have no inheritance with me" (Jn 13:8), He is effectively saying that Peter must yield to Jesus's act of love on the Cross in order for Peter to share in the divine life. See Martin and Wright, *Gospel of John*, 234–235.

53.   *Ratio Fundamentalis*, sec. 101, emphasis added.

54.   Guigo II, *Ladder of Monks and Twelve Meditations*, Cistercian Studies Series 48, trans. Edmund Colledge, OSA and James Walsh, SJ (Kalamazoo: Cistercian Publications, 1979).

55.   Ibid., 2, 67–68.

56.   Mariano Magrassi, OSB, *Praying the Bible: An Introduction to Lectio Divina*, trans. Edward Hagman, OFM, Cap. (Collegeville: Liturgical Press, 1998 [1990]), 89.

57.   *Verbum Domini*, sec. 87.

58.   Francis, "General Audience," 27 January 2021, https://www.vatican.va/content/francesco/en/ audiences/2021/documents/papa-francesco_20210127_udienza-generale.html (accessed January 29, 2022).

59.   Francis, Homily of the 3rd Sunday of Ordinary Time (Sunday of the Word of God), 23 January 2022, https://www.vatican.va/content/francesco/en/homilies/2022/documents/20220123_omelia-domenicadellaparoladidio.html (accessed January 29, 2022).

"To Derive Benefit from Every Part of the Text": Historical-Critical Study of Scripture and the Practice of Lectio Divina

Stephen Fahrig

I would like to make a plea for bringing to one's praying with the Scriptures an informed understanding of the text being prayed, for bringing the classroom into *lectio divina.* The purpose of this essay, therefore, is not so much to explore *lectio divina* itself as to consider one of the means by which seminarians and clergy can prepare to enter more fruitfully into the experience of *lectio,* namely preparatory study of the sacred text using insights from the historical-critical method of biblical interpretation.

At first glance, the juxtaposition of the terms "historical-critical method" (hereafter HCM) and "*lectio divina*" might seem an uneasy—if not downright oxymoronic—pairing. One is reminded of Tertullian's famous quip regarding the supposed incompatibility between philosophy and theology: "What has Athens to do with Jerusalem?" Actually, for many seminarians entering the theologate after a period of philosophy studies, the relationship between Athens and Jerusalem might be far more self-evident than that between the HCM and their life of prayer with the Sacred Scriptures.

In my twelve years of teaching Sacred Scripture in a seminary setting, my general experience has been that men arrive in my classroom with a generally negative attitude toward the HCM. When introducing the topic of biblical methodologies at the beginning of the semester, I regularly ask, "How many of you have a *positive* view of the historical-critical method?" In most years, only one or two students will raise their hands, usually with some hesitation. When I ask the inevitable follow-up question—"How many of you have a *negative* view of the historical-critical method?"—usually between half and two-thirds of the hands in the room rapidly shoot up. By contrast, when I ask similar questions about the canonical approach to interpretation, the student response is almost universally favorable toward that method.

Why this antipathy toward the HCM? Understood at its most basic level, this method (or set of methods, to be more precise) is simply an interpretive approach to Scripture that focuses especially on the original historical settings of the biblical books and what they meant in those contexts.[1] Given the Church's insistence that any interpretation of a biblical text must be based on its literal sense,[2] the necessity of employing historical-critical methodologies should appear obvious. Indeed, the Pontifical Biblical Commission in its 1993 document *Interpretation of the Bible in the Church* referred to the HCM as "the indispensable method for the scientific study of the meaning of ancient texts,"[3] a claim that would be echoed by the chief architect of the document, Joseph Ratzinger, during his later pontificate as Benedict XVI.[4] However, as Benedict himself would point out, the HCM is, despite its "indispensable" character, inherently limited: "It considers the individual books of Scripture in the context of their historical period, and then analyzes them further according to their sources. The unity of all these writings as one 'Bible,' however, is not something it can recognize as an immediate historical datum."[5] Practiced in isolation, the HCM can (and often does) treat the Bible as simply a historical artifact.

To any person of faith who has found him- or herself called to the ecclesial vocation of seminary theology and undertaken the necessary studies to attain a licentiate or a doctorate, Benedict's cautions (and the concerns of our students) ought to resonate. I think it is safe to say that many of us have encountered less-than edifying uses of the HCM in the classroom during our own studies and later, in our regular engagement with biblical commentaries in our research and class preparation. At their best, many applications of the HCM can often seem to be overly dry, technical, and irrelevant to nourishing a view of Scripture as the Word of God. At their worst, they can actually pose a threat to such a view, presenting a rationalist conception of the Bible that leaves no room for the supernatural either in its composition or in the salvific events that it purports to relate. While I was fortunate to have been spared the most egregious abuses of the HCM during my studies, I nevertheless can identify with the trepidation of the seminarians whom I teach. Who among us has not, for example, taken an Old Testament course that amounted to little more than a historical survey of the religion and politics of the Ancient Near East, or waded through a scholarly commentary that was heavily laden with insights from source and form criticism but bereft of genuine theology? Such lopsided applications of historical-critical methodology, divorced from a faith perspective that sees Christ as the fulfillment of the Old Testament, can, to use a bad pun I adopted a few years back, turn biblical "exegesis" into "Exit, Jesus."

The reality is that the HCM can be misused. However, the misuse of a thing does not negate its proper use. Since 1943, the Catholic Church has consistently recommended the use of historical-critical methodologies in order to arrive at a full and sound interpretation of biblical texts.[6] Indeed, the sixth edition of the *Program of Priestly Formation* in essence requires the use of the HCM—in conjunction with other interpretive methodologies—by citing those paragraphs of the *Catechism* and *Dei Verbum* that insist upon attending to the original meaning of a biblical text when engaging in the work of exegesis.[7]

It is, therefore, evident that the Church sees value in the HCM as a legitimate form of exegesis, so long as it is employed from a perspective of faith and in union with canonical criticism and other synchronic approaches to the biblical text. But can it be useful in praying with the Scriptures? Can there be a harmonious union between the "Athens" of the HCM and the "Jerusalem" of *lectio divina*?

I believe that there can. Indeed, if we take Jesus's Parable of the Sower seriously, then we must use every available means to prepare the "ground" of our hearts and minds so as to make them fertile soil for the seeds of the Word that our Lord wants to plant within us. In the remainder of this essay, I will first offer some thoughts as to why a moderate use of historical methodology might be needed to facilitate a more fruitful engagement with the Bible in prayer. I will then offer a concrete example, drawn from Isaiah 7, of how it might do so.

The Sources of Daily Lectio and the Value of Preparatory Study

As a preliminary step in this direction, let us first consider the content of *lectio* as it is practiced by many seminarians and clergy. Authorities on the spiritual life and the practice of *lectio divina* have differing opinions on how practitioners of sacred reading should approach their task. One such difference centers on the choice of reading for one's ongoing, daily commitment to *lectio divina*. Many spiritual masters (admittedly, far more advanced in the spiritual life than I) would insist upon the methodical reading-and-praying-through of an entire biblical book, from beginning to end. This is in distinction to an approach to *lectio* that would draw upon the daily cycle of Scripture readings found, for instance, in the Lectionary and in the Office of Readings of the Liturgy of the Hours.

Let me be clear: I am an enthusiastic advocate of ongoing, systematic prayer with and study of the *entire* Bible. I wholeheartedly agree with Peter Williamson, who in a recent essay emphasized the vital importance of regularly reading the Scriptures in their entirety. Williamson's words deserve quotation in full:

> My experience teaching Scripture to seminarians has demonstrated that the daily reading of the Lectionary and Liturgy of the Hours alone does not lead to familiarity with the biblical books, since the selections are not read in their contexts. Only a repeated lectio continua brings about the kind of familiarity that enables a pastoral minister to be fluent in preaching, teaching, or counseling from sacred Scripture.[8]

Williamson is correct in his assertions. A study by Father Felix Just, SJ concluded that only 13.5 percent of the Old Testament (not including the Psalms) and 71.5 percent of the New Testament is read at Mass in the Sunday and weekday lectionaries over the course of three years.[9] When one adds the content of the Office of Readings in the Liturgy of the Hours, the percentage of the Old Testament read in the Liturgy increases but not significantly. In light of these statistics, I have begun making a point of strongly encouraging my seminary students to develop this practice of "lectio continua" so as to develop an intimate familiarity with the whole deposit of Sacred Scripture.

Nevertheless, it is my experience that, for a respectable portion of seminarians and ordained clergy, it is the daily readings set forth by the Church in the Lectionary and in the Breviary's Office of Readings that often serve as the content of their daily *lectio*. In fact, when I was discerning a priestly vocation myself, I once had a spiritual director who strongly encouraged me to turn to the Office of Readings as a primary source for my daily prayer, absent any planned engagement with a specific biblical book or a movement of the Holy Spirit that might lead me to meditate on something else on a given day. That advice has stuck with me, and as I am a layman now in formation for the permanent diaconate, the Office of Readings (or one of the Mass readings of the day) often continues to be my first choice as a resource for *lectio divina*.

Having said that, prior to undertaking advanced biblical studies, I often found that my attempts to pray fruitfully with texts in the Breviary or Lectionary (especially from the Old Testament) were frustrated by a lack of familiarity with the historical, cultural, and geographical world of Israel and the

Ancient Near East. I doubt if my experience was unique. There are a fair number of Old Testament passages in the Breviary that can be intimidating for those who are unfamiliar with (or have forgotten!) its history and geography. For instance, during the eleventh week of Ordinary Time, the Church sets forth for us in the Office of Readings a selection of passages from the Book of Judges. On Monday of that week, we read the very graphic and compelling story of Jael's brutal murder of the Canaanite general Sisera (Jgs 4:1–24). Before we ever get to the "exciting" part of the story (in which Jael drives a tent peg through the unfortunate Sisera's skull), we are bombarded with a bewildering assortment of personal and geographic names:

> The Israelites again did what was evil in the sight of the Lord; Ehud was dead. So the Lord sold them into the power of the Canaanite king, Jabin, who reigned in Hazor. The general of his army was Sisera, who lived in Harosheth-ha-goiim. But the Israelites cried out to the Lord; for with his nine hundred iron chariots Jabin harshly oppressed the Israelites for twenty years. At that time the prophet Deborah, wife of Lappidoth, was judging Israel. She used to sit under Deborah's palm tree, between Ramah and Bethel in the mountain region of Ephraim, where the Israelites came up to her for judgment. She had Barak, son of Abinoam, summoned from Kedesh of Naphtali. She said to him, "This is what the Lord, the God of Israel, commands: Go, march against Mount Tabor, and take with you ten thousand men from Naphtali and Zebulun. I will draw Sisera, the general of Jabin's army, out to you at the Wadi Kishon, together with his chariots and troops, and I will deliver them into your power." (Jgs 4:1–7)[10]

I can vividly remember reading this passage as a young seminarian, poorly versed in the people and places of the Ancient Near East, and feeling overwhelmed and frustrated. In rapid succession, I was exposed to Jabin, Sisera, Harosheth-ha-goiim, Lappidoth, Ramah, Bethel, Ephraim, Abinoam, and the Wadi Kishon—to name but some of the people and places cited in this text. No matter how compelling the subsequent account of Jael's victory over Sisera might have been, I recall feeling "stuck" in the earlier proclamation of personal and place names, wondering who these people were, where the action of the story was located, why on earth it should matter to me as a twenty-first-century seminarian, and whether I ought not to just count my losses and move on to the second reading from the Church Fathers and hope to find some spiritual nourishment there.

To cite another example: during the Advent season, the Church appropriately exposes us to a generous sampling of the oracles in the book of Isaiah. This prophetic text, famously dubbed "the fifth gospel" for its many passages that point to the conception, birth, life, and Death of Jesus Christ, is indeed fitting reading for the liturgical season in which we celebrate the coming of our incarnate Lord. Nevertheless, despite the bold assertion of Advent Preface II in the Eucharistic Liturgy that "all the oracles of the prophets foretold him," I can recall many instances in my years of formation in which I attentively prayed my way through the Isaian pericopes in the Breviary, hoping to find some kind of explicit or implicit connection with the birth of my Savior, only to be presented instead with bewildering references to "Sela across the desert" (Is 16:1), refugees from Moab (Is 16:2–4), and woes pronounced on someone or something called "Ariel" (Is 29:1). On a happy day in which I might find one verse out of twenty or more that had an obvious Christological connection, I might fixate on that verse while dismissing the remainder of the passage as cryptic and irrelevant. And yet, I could not help wondering . . . was not *all* of this text the Word of God? And did the Church really want me to fix my attention only on one or two verses, while neglecting the immense riches that were undoubtedly contained in the remainder?

Over time, particularly after pursuing advanced Scripture studies while working on my licentiate and doctorate, I began to see the value of an appropriate use of the HCM in unearthing the buried treasures found in these passages. I would eventually come across the following observation by Saint Cyril of Jerusalem, which perfectly encapsulated the instinct that I had been developing for many years. His words, written many centuries before the rise of modern historical study of Scripture, are nonetheless strikingly relevant to our present discussion:

> The word of the holy prophets is always difficult to surmise. It is filled with hidden meanings and is pregnant with announcements of divine mysteries. . . . Those who want to expound these subtle matters must be diligent, I believe, to work in a logical way to thoroughly examine all of the symbols in the text *to gain spiritual insight*. First, the interpreter must determine the *historical meaning* and then interpret the spiritual meaning, in order for readers *to derive benefit from every part of the text*. The exposition must be clearly seen to be complete in every way.[11]

Saint Cyril's directives for biblical interpretation are wise, balanced, and worthy of imitation by every student of Sacred

Scripture. Without in any way denying the importance of a canonical and Christological approach to the Old Testament ("the spiritual meaning"), he rightly emphasizes the need to "determine the historical meaning" of a passage in order to "derive benefit from every part of the text." As an example of how his suggestion might be put into practice—and in due course, applied to prayer with Scripture—let us consider a significant passage from the book of Isaiah.

Isaiah 7 as a Model for Preparatory Study

Perhaps one of the best-known verses of the Old Testament is the "Emmanuel prophecy" found in Isaiah 7:14. Proclaimed liturgically during the Advent season and on the solemnity of the Annunciation, and famously set to music by Handel in his *Messiah*, this single verse is beloved by many Christians: "Behold, the virgin shall be with child and bear a son, and they shall name him Emmanuel" (Mt 1:23). Its Christian significance stems in large part from Matthew's use of it in his infancy narrative, where he cites it as a prophecy of the virginal conception of Jesus through the power of the Holy Spirit (Mt 1:18, 23).[12] When read in light of the unique circumstances of Jesus's birth, the verse does attain profound importance as a messianic prophecy. But, to return to one of the key points with which I began this essay, if contemporary Catholic readers focus exclusive attention on this one line of Scripture while neglecting the wider passage that surrounds it, they might find themselves missing out on a lot of valuable insights that could enhance their experience of *lectio*. They might, in fact, even miss some of the important connections the Holy Spirit might be inviting them to make between the passage and their lives.

Indeed, a Catholic priest or seminarian approaching Isaiah 7 in, say, the context of the Office of Readings may well be distracted by all of the other verses that precede and follow Isaiah 7:14 if his only focus is on that particular verse![13] This might especially be the case if one uses an alternative translation (permitted by the General Instruction of the Liturgy of the Hours) such as the Revised Standard Version, New Revised Standard Version, or the New American Bible Revised Edition, which replace the familiar "virgin" of 7:14 with "young woman." The pivotal Emmanuel prophecy in verse 14 is preceded by thirteen verses of narrative focused on the prophet Isaiah's interactions with Ahaz, the intransigent and worldly king of Judah. We learn that the kings of Syria and *Israel* have joined forces to wage a military campaign against Jerusalem (a confusing scenario in itself, unless one knows or recalls that "Israel" in this instance refers to the northern kingdom that emerged after the death of Solomon, not the united kingdom that had Jerusalem as its capital). Why are Israel and Syria seeking a war with Judah? Why are they trying to overthrow Ahaz and replace him with a puppet king (Is 7:6)? Why is King Ahaz so resistant to Isaiah's generous offer of a divine sign (Is 7:10–12)? Why does Isaiah say that "Emmanuel" will "learn to reject evil and choose good" if this is a prophecy about Jesus Christ? Above all, why should any priest or seminarian genuinely care about the answers to these questions?

In part, the answer is that a solid historical understanding of King Ahaz and his circumstances can actually better help us to appreciate the relevance of the Emmanuel prophecy to the conception of Jesus. This is especially the case when the respective responses of Ahaz and the Virgin Mary to God are contrasted liturgically on those days where their stories are paired in the Lectionary.[14] In its original context, the story of Ahaz in Isaiah 7 is a commentary on an individual's capacity (or lack thereof) to trust in God alone rather than in human strength. For readers of Isaiah, both ancient and modern, King Ahaz epitomizes a *lack* of trust in the Lord. He was leading the kingdom of Judah at a time when the Assyrian Empire was growing in strength and proving to be a threat to its smaller neighbors. Two of those small nations—Syria and Israel—had formed a coalition to oppose the advance of Assyrian power and wanted Judah to join them. Ahaz refused to do so, and, as we learn in Isaiah 7:1, found himself on the receiving end of a military invasion by their forces.

Why had Ahaz refused to join this military coalition? Was it because he devoutly held to the belief that YHWH, the God of Israel, would protect Jerusalem and its Davidic king and, therefore, he need not fear the military power of Assyria? Absolutely not! As Isaiah knew (and, assuming our familiarity with a parallel narrative in 2 Kings 16, we readers would also know), Ahaz had already chosen to make an alliance with the very Assyrian Empire that was threatening his country:

> Then Rezin, king of Aram, and Pekah, son of Remaliah, king of Israel, came up to Jerusalem to attack it. Although they besieged Ahaz, they were unable to do battle. . . . Meanwhile, Ahaz sent messengers to Tiglath-pileser, king of Assyria, with the plea: "*I am your servant and your son. Come up and rescue me from the power of the king of Aram and the king of Israel, who are attacking me.*" Ahaz took the silver and gold that were in the house of the Lord and in the treasuries of the king's house and sent

them as a present to the king of Assyria. (2 Kgs 16:5, 7–8, emphasis added)

There is a tragic irony in the words of Ahaz to the Assyrian emperor: "I am your servant and your son." As a descendant of King David, Ahaz should have been familiar with the promise made to David by God via the prophet Nathan: "I will raise up your offspring after you, sprung from your loins, and I will establish his kingdom. He it is who shall build a house for my name, and I will establish his royal throne forever. *I will be a father to him, and he shall be a son to me*" (2 Sm 7:12b–14, emphasis added).[15] Ahaz, who appears to have failed Covenant Theology 101, has failed to understand himself as a beloved son of God, an heir to the Davidic covenant promises, and has turned instead to the king of Assyria as his "adoptive father."

Despite Ahaz's profound failure to embrace his sonship, God does not give up on His wayward child; indeed, He brings about the meeting between Isaiah and the king in order to encourage Ahaz to trust in His divine providence. The Lord makes it clear through His prophet that Ahaz has an opportunity, in the midst of this political/military crisis, to grow in virtue by placing his trust in God. Unfortunately, the king is the embodiment of pragmatism and more easily trusts the Assyrian king he can see to the God he cannot see. Nevertheless, in verses 10–17, we are told that the Lord dispatches Isaiah to Ahaz a second time, offering the ruler another chance to place his confidence where it truly belongs. This time round, the prophet offers the king an opportunity that most people would be loath to refuse: "If you are having trouble trusting in God, ask a sign of him—*any* sign at all, and God will give it to you!" Ahaz, however, is set on his predetermined course of action, so, in an ostentatious display of false piety, he refuses, saying in essence: "I would *never dream* of putting God to the test!" Ahaz does not want to ask for a sign because he is afraid that God will actually give him one! He has already made up his mind to throw in his lot with the Assyrians, and he does not want anyone telling him what to do.

Isaiah now loses all patience with the king and gives him a piece of his prophetic mind. "So, you don't want a sign? Too bad! You're gonna get one anyway. Look—the *'almah* is pregnant, and is going to have a son, and he will be called Emmanuel!" I have left the Hebrew word *'almah* untranslated here because its meaning is ambiguous. It could refer to a woman who has never had sexual relations—that is, a virgin—or it could simply refer to a young woman of childbearing age. It is used in both senses elsewhere in the Old Testament. Within the original setting of this prophecy, we might picture Isaiah pointing beyond Ahaz to a woman and saying, "Look over there; this woman is going to bear a child who will symbolize God's presence among us." In fact, many exegetes see an *initial* fulfillment of the "Emmanuel" prophecy in the birth of Hezekiah, the son of King Ahaz (without necessarily denying an *ultimate* fulfillment in the virginal conception of Jesus).[16]

Hezekiah, in stark contrast to his father, was remembered by the biblical writers for his great trust in God, and for undertaking a sweeping religious reform during his reign as king. He restricted the worship of YHWH to the Temple in Jerusalem. Outside the book of Isaiah, we find a very positive presentation of Hezekiah in the so-called Deuteronomistic history. In 2 Kings 18, we read that "He did what was right in the Lord's sight, just as David his father had done. . . . He put his trust in the Lord, the God of Israel" (2 Kgs 18:3, 5). Indeed, Hezekiah is one of only three kings besides David who receives a thoroughly complimentary evaluation from the Deuteronomists. Moreover, the author of 2 Kings goes on to say of Hezekiah, "The Lord was with him" (2 Kgs 18:7). Thanks to Hezekiah's trust and obedience, Israel was saved from the threat of the Assyrians during his reign. For many citizens of Judah in the eighth century, perhaps it did seem as if Hezekiah's reign was a time in which "God is with us," as Isaiah had predicted. However, like all mere mortals, Hezekiah died. His successor, Manasseh, proved to be one of the worst kings in the entire Davidic bloodline. He not only undid Hezekiah's religious reforms but indulged in the worst abominations of pagan worship, including child sacrifice.[17] In short, whatever blessings came from God to Judah during Hezekiah's reign, they were short lived. In its original historical context, the promise of "Emmanuel" remained unfulfilled, awaiting a future realization.

Centuries after Hezekiah's time, we learn in the Gospel of Luke that the angel Gabriel was sent to a virgin in the town of Nazareth who is engaged to Joseph, a member of the house of David. According to Matthew's genealogy of Jesus, Joseph was a direct descendant of the same Davidic bloodline that brought forth the kings Ahaz, Hezekiah, and Manasseh. Presented with a perplexing announcement, Mary is troubled; and she even asks the angel a legitimate question ("How can this be?"). In the end, however, she trustingly places her life at the disposal of God and His plan for the salvation of the human race. Consider now the stark difference between Mary and Ahaz. Ahaz disavowed his royal sonship and declared himself to be the son and servant of the Assyrian emperor. Mary, by contrast, described herself as the "handmaid"—literally, the *slave*—of the Lord. It is here that the insights gained from a historical reading of Isaiah 7 can be fruitfully combined with a canonical reading of the passage in light of Luke's story of the Annunciation. Knowing something of the personality of Ahaz and the historical circumstances in which he acted can prepare the reader of Sacred Scripture to draw a clear comparison and contrast between this untrusting Judahite king and Mary, the ideal disciple who places all her trust in God.

The fact that Isaiah's oracles were spoken in a specific historical context does not preclude a more transcendent meaning in light of salvation history. The Holy Spirit who inspired the authors of Sacred Scripture was certainly capable of arranging for the words of prophets such as Isaiah to contain multiple levels of meaning. In the text we are considering, an initial prediction about a young woman giving birth in Isaiah's own time would portend and find ultimate fulfillment in the birth of another child, a child whose presence in this world would truly be that of Emmanuel, "God with us." It is appropriate to look again at the words of Pope Benedict:

> Historical-critical interpretation of a text seeks to discover the precise sense the words were intended to convey at their time and place of origin. But . . . it is necessary to keep in mind that any human utterance of a certain weight contains *more than the author may have been immediately aware of at the time.* When a word *transcends the moment in which it is spoken,* it carries within itself a *"deeper value."*[18]

Bringing it Together: Applying the Fruits of the Historical-
Critical Method to Lectio with Isaiah 7

At this point, readers might be saying to themselves, "Okay, this is fascinating historical and theological background on King Ahaz, but what does it have to do with me? It's not like I'm a spiritual advisor to the president of the United States . . . " Having looked at the interpretation of Isaiah chapter 7—particularly verse 14 with its Emmanuel prophecy—from both a historical and canonical perspective, I will conclude by looking at how a man in the seminary might apply this knowledge about the passage to his personal *lectio*.

Let us consider the following scenario. Ben is a seminarian who has had a rough summer assignment between his second and third years of theology studies. Some aspects of this difficult experience have led him to question whether he still feels called to ordained ministry, but he is reluctant to fully acknowledge his uncertainty. When Ben's assignment is over and he has a couple of weeks off before school starts up again, he goes to meet with his spiritual director. After hearing the young man's concerns, the director suggests that perhaps Ben should pray about asking his bishop and his rector to do a pastoral year, to allow for greater discernment prior to his ordination to the diaconate. Immediately, the seminarian feels a wall of resistance building up within him. "I know I'm called to the priesthood," he says to himself. "I've known since I was ten years old. My family is already preparing for my diaconate ordination in May. And my eighty-six-year-old grandmother, who lit up like a Christmas tree the day I told her I was going to the seminary, was just diagnosed with dementia. If I put off my ordination for a whole year, she may not even know who I am by then, if she's even still alive. No way am I doing a pastoral year." This is what is going through Ben's mind. Outwardly, however, he smiles weakly at his director and promises to "pray about it." But his mind is made up. And since his director's counsel is strictly "internal forum," well . . . perhaps he thinks, "My formators aren't going to hear about this. And I don't need to tell them. The stuff that happened this summer really just amounts to a few bumps on the road. I'll be fine."

This is a case in which an understanding of the historical context of Scripture might be a powerful means by which the Holy Spirit might hold up a mirror to this young man's situation. Suppose that the next day, our seminarian is praying the Office of Readings, and lo and behold, there is Isaiah chapter 7, with good old King Ahaz pursuing his own path and refusing to listen to the spiritual counsel of the prophet Isaiah.[19] Ben, who has relished his Scripture studies and not only knows Ahaz's background but is familiar with the Lectionary's juxtaposition of Ahaz and Hezekiah on the solemnity of the Annunciation, begins reflecting on the contrast between the king of Judah and the Blessed Mother. (Given that the second reading in the Office that day is from a homily of Saint Bernard on the Blessed Virgin Mary, this association might, perhaps, be inevitable.) Like Ahaz, Mary was presented with an opportunity to trust God in the midst of circumstances that were, frankly, bizarre. Imagine being a young woman and having an angel come to you to tell you that—guess what—you are going to be the mother of the long-awaited Messiah and—hold on to your hat—you are going to conceive the child without the help of a human father! In spite of the incredibly challenging situation in which she finds herself, Mary, nonetheless, chose to place her trust in God. As a result, the greatest blessing in all of human history took place with her cooperation—the Word became flesh in and lived among us. Emmanuel, "God is with us," came to dwell with the human race in the person of Jesus of Nazareth.

As Ben prays with these texts in the Office, he might ask himself: "Am I going to be an Ahaz who refuses to listen to the voice of God, speaking to me, in this case through my spiritual director, or am I going to emulate the Blessed Virgin Mary, who responded obediently to God's will even though it meant a radical change in the direction of her life?" After spending some time in prayer, reflecting upon the diverse responses of Ahaz and Mary to God's invitation in their lives, he is convicted by the realization that he ought to take his director's advice and have a conversation with his bishop about doing a pastoral year.

A few short years later, having weathered the storms of his vocational crisis and been ordained to the priesthood, *Father* Ben now finds himself preaching on the Solemnity of the Annunciation. He has at hand a set of Lectionary texts that are profoundly meaningful for him because he has studied them, prayed them, and allowed them to influence his life. He is now able to easily draw out the contrasts between Ahaz and Mary for his congregation: "We all need to ask ourselves at times, 'Am I really open to God's will? Or am I just following my own path? Am I a Mary who trusts in God, or an Ahaz who trusts in my own resources for strength and guidance? Do I listen to the voice of God as it is relayed to me through Scripture, Church teaching, my spiritual director, etc.?' There is a little bit of Ahaz in all of us. Wounded by original sin, we all have a tendency to follow our own will instead of God's will, to say 'I did it my way.' May God grant us the grace to shun the prideful self-reliance that characterized King Ahaz and instead imitate the humble trust of Our Lady."

As this illustration suggests, an appropriate use of historical study of the Scriptures can greatly enhance one's capacity to receive helpful spiritual insights when engaging in *lectio divina*. Had our seminarian in this scenario never delved into the story of King Ahaz and the situation that he faced in Judah in the eighth century BC, he might have never recognized the "Ahaz in himself" when praying with Isaiah 7. Because he was equipped with an awareness of the passage's historical context, however, the Holy Spirit was able to work with him in a powerful way.

Conclusion

The historical-critical study of Sacred Scripture is, despite the misuse that has been made of it by some "rationalist" exegetes since its inception, an invaluable and "indispensable" component of biblical interpretation. Its value is not limited to the academy, however, as the foregoing observations have sought to illustrate. When regularly incorporated into a seminarian or cleric's ongoing routine of Scripture study, the historical-critical method can yield insights that later bear fruit in the practice of *lectio*. Prayerful attentiveness to these insights can enable the man who prays with Scripture to "derive benefit from every part" of a biblical passage, deepening his capacity to receive all that the Spirit desires to offer him through the inspired Word.

NOTES

1. See Pontifical Biblical Commission, *Interpretation of the Bible in the Church* (Boston: Pauline Books and Media, 1993), 35–42.

2. *Catechism of the Catholic Church* (Washington, DC: USCCB Publishing, 2000), sec. 116, quoting Saint Thomas Aquinas, *Summa Theologica* I, 1, 10, *ad* I.

3. Pontifical Biblical Commission, *Interpretation of the Bible in the Church* (1993), sec. 35. The document continues: "Holy Scripture, inasmuch as it is the 'word of God in human language,' has been composed by human authors in all its various parts and in all the sources that lie behind them. Because of this, its proper understanding not only admits the use of this method but actually requires it."

4. See, for example, Benedict XVI, *Verbum Domini* (2010), sec. 34–37; *Jesus of Nazareth: From the Baptism in the Jordan to the Transfiguration* (New York: Doubleday, 2007), xiv–xviii.

5. Benedict XVI, *Jesus of Nazareth*, xvii.

6. To cite just a couple of examples, Pope Pius XII in his groundbreaking encyclical *Divino Afflante Spiritu* strongly encouraged the use of modern critical methodologies, stating "Let the interpreter then, with all care and without neglecting any light derived from recent research, endeavor to determine the peculiar character and circumstances of the sacred writer, the age in which he lived, the sources written or oral to which he had recourse and the forms of expression he employed. . . . the interpreter must, as it were, go back wholly in spirit to those remote centuries of the East" (Pius XII, *Divino Afflante Spiritu* [1943], sec. 33). *Dei Verbum* would go on to insist that "since God speaks in Sacred Scripture through men in human fashion, the interpreter of Sacred Scripture, in order to see clearly what God wanted to communicate to us, should carefully investigate what meaning the sacred writers really intended, and what God wanted to manifest by means of their words" (Vatican Council II, *Dei Verbum* [1965], sec. 12).

7. United States Conference of Catholic Bishops (USCCB), *Program of Priestly Formation*, 6th ed. no. 324 (Washington, DC: USCCB, 2022), sec. 70.

8. Peter S. Williamson, "Implications of the New Evangelization for Priestly Ministry," in *The Revelation of Your Words: The New Evangelization and the Role of the Seminary Professor of Sacred Scripture*, ed. Kevin Zilverberg and Scott Carl (Saint Paul, MN: Saint Paul Seminary Press, 2021), 16–17.

9. Felix Just, SJ, "Lectionary Statistics," https://catholic-resources.org/Lectionary/Statistics.htm.

10. Unless otherwise noted, all Scripture quotations are taken from the *New American Bible, Revised Edition*.

11. Cyril of Alexandria, *Commentary on Isaiah*, Introduction, cited in John Bergsma and Brant Pitre, *A Catholic Introduction to the Bible: The Old Testament* (San Francisco: Ignatius Press, 2018), 754–55, emphasis added.

12. Matthew cites the verse in its Greek translation, which renders the ambiguous Hebrew word '*almah* (which, as we will see, can mean "young woman" or "maiden") unambiguously as *parthenos*, which means "virgin."

13. Of course, it could be reasonably objected that in *lectio*, one's prayer might simply focus on one verse, or even one word, from a longer passage of Scripture. This is undoubtedly true, and my purpose here is not to suggest that a lack of appreciation for historical context in Scripture is an impediment to the Holy Spirit's power to move the heart and mind of the one praying. Rather, my intention is to make the case that the more one knows about a given biblical text, the more avenues the Spirit is able to open up for our spiritual insight.

14. Isaiah 7:10–14 and Luke 1:26–38 are read together in the Liturgy on two significant occasions: on the Solemnity of the Annunciation (March 25) and on December 20, one of the final days of the Advent season leading up to Christmas.

15. In its fullest sense, this passage applies to Jesus Christ as the unique Son of God; but in its original setting, it would have been understood in reference to David's son Solomon and all of his successors as king.

16. Bergsma and Pitre, in their recent survey of the Old Testament, offer a good example of a balanced exegetical approach to this text, which allows for both an initial fulfillment in Isaiah's time and an ultimate fulfillment with the coming of Christ: "In the case of Isaiah 7:14, the preliminary fulfillment of the 'Immanuel' child may well have been Hezekiah son of Ahaz, and the '*almah* may have been Abijah, a young bride of Ahaz (2 Chron 29:1), who was probably not yet intimate with the king. Before Hezekiah was a young man, the Syro-Ephraimite threat had evaporated. . . . Hezekiah was born of a 'maiden' ('*almah*) in the usual manner, but later one would be born of a mother who remained a maiden before, during, and after his birth. Hezekiah was 'Immanuel' ('God with us') in a mediated sense: his righteous reign was a sign of God's closeness to his people. But later one would be born who was truly 'God with us' in a literal sense. Applied to Hezekiah, the poetry and language of these oracles is hyperbolic: complete fulfillment awaits another." See Bergsma and Pitre, *Catholic Introduction to the Bible*, 748–49.

17. See 2 Kings 21:1–18.

18. Benedict XVI, *Jesus of Nazareth*, xix–xx, emphasis added.

19. Isaiah 7:1–17 is read in the Office of Readings on Tuesday of the Twentieth Week in Ordinary Time, which typically falls in the latter half of August.

ROYAL FORMATION, DISCIPLESHIP FORMATION, CLERGY FORMATION

LLANE B. BRIESE

The Church's magisterium has increasingly reminded clergy that they must be deeply formed by the Word of God. Like the Blessed Mother, we clergy are called and consecrated by God and sent out to His people to serve. In the Sacrament of Holy Orders, the Holy Spirit overshadows us so that we may fulfill our divine mission. Like Mary, we must welcome the Word and let it take root in our lives.[1]

For good reason, therefore, Pope Benedict XVI reminded us in his 2010 Apostolic Exhortation *Verbum Domini* that "[b]ishops, priests, and deacons can hardly think that they are living out their vocation and mission apart from a decisive and renewed commitment to sanctification, one of whose pillars is contact with God's word."[2] Similarly, Pope Francis has reminded clergy, charged with the sublime work of preaching the liturgical homily, that their work in the pulpit only has value if the preacher has first welcomed the Word:

> What is essential is that the preacher be certain that God loves him, that Jesus Christ has saved him and that his love

always has the last word. Encountering such beauty, he will often feel that his life does not glorify God as it should, and he will sincerely desire to respond more fully to so great a love. Yet if he does not take time to hear God's word with an open heart, if he does not allow it to touch his life, to challenge him, to impel him, and if he does not devote time to pray with that word, then he will indeed be a false prophet, a fraud, a shallow impostor. . . . The Lord wants to make use of us as living, free and creative beings who let his word enter their own hearts before then passing it on to others. Christ's message must truly penetrate and possess the preacher, not just intellectually but in his entire being.[3]

In my dual role as a seminary Scripture professor and formation advisor, I find that seminarians and candidates for the permanent diaconate intuitively grasp this importance. They generally value Marian devotion, silent prayer before the Most Blessed Sacrament, and *lectio divina*. That said, they often struggle to connect what they learn in their biblical courses to prayer and pastoral practice, consistent with what the Synod of Bishops indicated in 2008, that seminarians need guidance to see the connection between exegesis and personal prayer.[4] In a nutshell, the skills gleaned from academic courses on biblical exegesis form the foundation for the first stage of *lectio divina*: sound exegesis furnishes a most probing *lectio*, which sets the stage for a rich *meditatio, oratio,* and *contemplatio*.

Without a sufficiently exacting exegesis, the grand edifice of prayer will lack sufficient foundation; without a commitment to meditative and contemplative prayer, exegesis fails to attain its proper aim. Indeed, as Konrad Schaefer recently explained most ably,

Without the exegetical exercise, the Bible risks being reduced to pious platitudes or aphorisms. But in an analogous manner, without faith and insight, by which the spirit of the text speaks for the hearer of today and reflects on the theological sense for the present life of the Church, the contact with the Word of God will be reduced to antiquarianism.[5]

Exegesis—"a guided tour" of the biblical text[6]—allows the reader to approach the Lord in prayer and ascend to the heights of meditation, prayer, and contemplation.

Recent exegetical developments have provided readers of faith with new tools to appreciate not just the history and geography implicated by the text, but also its literary artistry and beauty. Beyond the insights gleaned from narrative analysis and studies into the poetic character of various texts,[7] attention to how the text seeks to inspire, persuade, and influence its reader—what literary scholars call narrative rhetoric[8]—allows us to appreciate how the Holy Spirit, through the inspired human author's literary choices, not only calls us to believe the truth but also moves us to goodness and beauty.

Although I shall neither enter into the theoretical foundations of narrative rhetoric nor employ much of its specialized vocabulary in this essay, two of its concepts will bear fruit in helping us appreciate the value of sound exegesis for uncovering God's subtle movements on the Sacred Page and bringing them to prayer in *lectio divina*: ideological rhetoric and aesthetic rhetoric.[9] As rhetoric refers to how a text influences its reader, ideological rhetoric seeks to persuade a reader that a given proposition is true or false, whereas aesthetic rhetoric seeks to move a reader to take a text seriously as a member of the literary genre to which it belongs. For example, the Stations of the Cross—a story, even if told only by pictures—persuade the person who prays them, either a reader of a book or a viewer of the scenes depicted visually, that Jesus truly suffered; this persuasive effect is an example of ideological rhetoric because it moves a viewer to believe a truth. However, the same Stations of the Cross may also pull at the heartstrings of viewers, moving them to tears as they consider the pain the Lord endured; these interior movements that direct the human mind to invest time and energy into the Stations of the Cross exemplify aesthetic rhetoric. Along these lines, Seymour Chatman defines aesthetic rhetoric as "suasion to accept the form of the narrative as most appropriate to its content,"[10] and presents a vision:

> In my view, there are two narrative rhetorics, one concerned to suade me to accept the form of the work [that is, aesthetic rhetoric]; another, to suade me of a certain view of how things are in the real world [that is, ideological rhetoric]. The investigation of these two rhetorics and their interaction strikes me as a crucial project for students of literature and of film.[11]

Though Chatman's invitation to investigation may, at first glance, seem of only marginal relevance to *lectio divina* and clergy formation, attention to the divinely inspired literature of the Bible grants us access to perceive more fully the love of the God who reveals Himself in Sacred Scripture.

In this contribution, I shall apply these two categories of narrative rhetoric—ideological and aesthetic—to two different biblical passages, one from each Testament, both of which contain important parallels with clergy formation: King Solomon's royal formation to serve as monarch in 1 Kings 1–3 and the discipleship formation of Jesus's first followers in John 1–2. As we shall see, both Solomon and the disciples would receive individualized attention from a divine formator, and both would resist formation at times. Yet Solomon would eventually fail as king in his vocation to shepherd God's holy people,[12] whereas the disciples would emerge from the Passion and Resurrection with renewed vigor, ready to fulfill their mission as agents of the Word-Made-Flesh.[13] I shall present a few examples of how a close reading with attention to the rhetoric of the two narratives can form a solid foundation for *lectio divina*.

Royal Formation of King Solomon (1 Kgs 1–3)

We begin by looking at King Solomon, son of David and Bathsheba,[14] one of the Bible's most perplexing characters, known both for his manifold wisdom[15] and foolish behavior.[16] Compared to the Chronicler's history,[17] the Book of Kings[18] portrays Solomon as a villain, a man raised to the throne and blessed with a supernatural gift of wisdom but who squanders it due to a weakness for women and riches.[19] Ben Sira's centuries-later eulogy to the Hebrew heroes would characterize Solomon as a tragic figure[20] and strongly imply that he should be remembered as a wicked king.[21] Yet, he was a leader appointed over God's people who only received his vocation after receiving support from others—Bathsheba, the prophet Nathan, the priest Zadok, and the military commander Benaiah[22]—and then was consecrated king by a mystical anointing.[23] In the same way, all clergy are presented for ordination only upon the recommendation of others and receive their leadership role through the Sacrament of Holy Orders. Like Solomon, priests and bishops receive an anointing during the ordination rite. Solomon's experience of royal formation, thus, can prove instructive to men preparing to receive upon ordination, among the threefold *munera*, the *munus regendi* (duty of governing).

As we read the first three chapters of 1 Kings, which describe Solomon's ascent to Israel's throne, we immediately notice that the inspired author begins with a montage of events[24]: David, senile with age, can no longer effectively govern,[25] so one son, Adonijah, assumes the role of his successor by plotting with Joab, David's military henchman, and Abiathar, a longtime priest, and excluding Solomon, his half-brother, along with Zadok, Benaiah, and Nathan, among others.[26] As we read, we are gripped by suspense, wondering what Adonijah's sneakiness will cost him. The pace of action slows down as we hear the prophet Nathan's plan to resist Adonijah, a plan that requires Bathsheba to intercede on her son Solomon's behalf and for Nathan to support her appeal.[27] Notably, we hear about the plan as it is being hatched and then hear it a second time as the characters put it into practice.[28] It works exactly as desired, as senile David swears to fulfill an oath to Bathsheba to make Solomon king[29]—an oath otherwise unrecorded in the Bible—and gives orders to have Solomon installed on the throne,[30] a command that Zadok, Nathan, and Benaiah follow immediately.[31] The action, already slowed down significantly from the frenetic pace of the opening ten verses, further slows as the inspired author painstakingly narrates the manner in which Adonijah learns this news, repeating Solomon's anointing as king for the third time,[32] and flees to the horns of the altar in an attempt to claim asylum.[33] We first see the new king act on his own—up until this point others have acted on his behalf—when he successfully summons Adonijah, who pays homage to him.[34] All this time, we learn almost nothing about Solomon's personal characteristics; we have no idea whether his accession to the throne serves the long-term interests of Israel. We learn only in due time the tragic consequences of his kingship.

At this juncture, the suspense spikes: Will Solomon forgive Adonijah, or will he eliminate him as a rival to the throne? The inspired author holds us breathless by interrupting the story with an account of David's final instructions to his successor before death.[35] Only after David's appeal to Solomon to keep the Mosaic Law[36] and practical instructions to punish Joab, among other advice,[37] do we hear about Adonijah's own appeal for Bathsheba's intercession, which she grants.[38] Indeed, the inspired author milks the scene, pausing the relevant action to allow us to hear about the separate throne set at the king's right for Bathsheba, a seemingly inessential detail.[39] All these compositional choices exemplify aesthetic rhetoric; the reader is eager to hear what happens next.

Only when the furniture has been set in place can Bathsheba appeal to her son, the king: "There is one small favor I would ask of you. Do not refuse me" (1 Kgs 2:20).[40] Crucially, Solomon agrees, "Ask it, my mother, for I will not refuse you" (1 Kgs 2:20). Once he learns the "small favor"—that Adonijah be given Abishag the Shunamite, David's former nurse,[41] as a wife—Solomon angrily reneges: "May God do thus to me and more, if Adonijah has not spoken this word at the cost of his life" (1 Kgs 2:23). In a case of tragic irony in a scene that echoes Bathsheba's intercession to David on Solomon's behalf, Solomon, like David, invokes the Lord's name in a vow,[42] but at the cost of his half-brother's life. The inspired author then tips his hand: he narrates the death of Adonijah in a terse sentence—ten Hebrew words[43]—after multiple paragraphs of holding us in suspense after Adonijah's first attempt to claim asylum by grasping the horns of the altar.[44] The sacred writer wants us to invest more time into learning Solomon's decision-making than into hearing about the consequence for Adonijah's life, a choice that raises a point of ideological rhetoric: Solomon cares more about suppressing potential subversion than remaining true to his word. His later diplomatic choices—which will lead him to intermarry with foreigners and accommodate their foreign gods in opposition to the Mosaic Law[45]—will follow this weak personality trait. The inspired author, and thus the Holy Spirit, wants to persuade us readers that Solomon was a weak man and that we should avoid imitating his poor example.

Having shown himself to be faithless and power-hungry, Solomon wastes no time consolidating his power and punishing Adonijah's associates. He exiles the priest Abiathar to Anathoth,[46] executes Joab after he tries to cling to the horns of the altar as Adonijah had done,[47] and kills a third man—Shimei, who had once cursed David[48]—after he fails to abide by the terms of an ultimatum.[49] In ordering Shimei's execution, Solomon utters a line that will sound a tragic note by the end of the Book of Kings: "King Solomon shall be blessed, and David's throne shall be established before the Lord forever" (1 Kgs 2:45). This confident boast, while ultimately vindicated by Christ's messianic kingdom,[50] certainly would have sounded foolhardy during the Babylonian Exile.[51] After all this bloodshed, the inspired author can only conclude with a succinct summary: "And the royal power was established in Solomon's hand" (1 Kgs 2:46). To further accentuate Solomon's wretchedness, the inspired author then informs us that "Solomon intermarried with Pharoah, the king of Egypt, and took the daughter of Pharaoh into the city of David until he could finish building his house, the house of the Lord, and the wall surrounding Jerusalem" (1 Kgs 3:1, my translation from the Hebrew). Has he no shame? He not only intermarries—an act itself frowned upon in Deuteronomy and elsewhere in the Deuteronomistic History[52]—but he does so with Pharaoh's daughter, an act that undermines the very legitimacy of the monarchy and the security of the land it was instituted to safeguard.[53] The attentive reader repels from such an act, screaming at the king: "No, don't do that!" Indeed, Solomon's marital alliance with Pharaoh runs contrary to the purpose of the Exodus itself, that Israel would be free to worship its God free from Pharoah's power.[54] In all these actions—absent from the Roman Lectionary and Breviary[55]—Solomon shows himself a man of weak character, one we should suspect as we hear the subsequent tales of his reign.

The Lectionary does, however, present a gerrymandered portrait of Solomon as it presents his prayer for wisdom,[56] which does find favor with God[57] and leads him to judge wisely a difficult child-custody dispute.[58] Careful attention to its context ensures a proper interpretation: Solomon has the capacity to live his royal vocation well; he knows how to pray for the right gift, and he receives manifold grace from God. But then he squanders it. He conscripts forced labor "from all Israel" (1 Kgs 5:27). Although in at least one case, he draws forced laborers only from resident non-Israelites,[59] "the harsh servitude and the heavy yoke" (1 Kgs 12:4, 2 Chr 10:4) leave sufficient lingering resentment among Israelites that his subjects divide the nation shortly after his death when his successor promises only to increase the burden,[60] setting the stage for the nation's tragic unraveling.

Although the story of Solomon's royal formation has a tragic ending, it provides a fruitful *lectio divina*. Clergy, too, receive abundant grace from the Lord. They assume the leadership of God's holy people and accept a vocation to safeguard the whole community. The clerical state holds inherent power, which can be used well or poorly. To recall the shepherd metaphor often used in the Ancient Near East to describe kings, shepherds may either feed the lambs or eat the lambs; clergy may empty themselves after the pattern of Christ, whom they serve at the altar, or they may devour the people's resources and use them to serve their own selfish ends. King Solomon makes the latter choice; *lectio divina* on his story summons us to choose differently.

Discipleship Formation of Jesus's First Followers (John 1–2)

The choice to feed the lambs or eat the lambs appears not only in Solomon's story. Jesus will give three explicit commands to Peter at the conclusion of John's Gospel: "feed my lambs" (Jn 21:15), "tend my sheep" (Jn 21:16), "feed my sheep" (Jn 21:17). Although Peter's path from fisherman to shepherd was hardly smooth,[61] he too received formation from the Lord to be able to follow the Lord even where he would not want to go.[62] We do well, therefore, to reflect also on Peter's own discipleship formation in the Fourth Gospel, which begins with his first encounter with the Lord on the third day of Jesus's public ministry,[63] when Andrew brings him to Jesus.[64] The Lord gives him the name Cephas (Peter) and the next day visits his hometown, Bethsaida, where he meets Philip and Nathanael, who confesses Jesus as "Son of God" and "King of Israel" (Jn

1:49). As lofty as these titles may seem, Jesus promises to show Nathanael—and the other first followers, by extension—"greater things" (Jn 1:50). These greater things begin a few days later when Jesus turns water into wine at the wedding of Cana,[65] thus revealing His glory and eliciting faith from the disciples.[66] After "only a few days" in Capernaum,[67] Jesus and the disciples travel to Jerusalem for the first of three Passovers recorded in John's Gospel.[68]

The discipleship formation jumps into another gear with this episode in Jerusalem. Although the story is famous for Jesus's actions in cleansing the temple area of profiteers from the religious activities taking place there, the Evangelist shows us by his manner of storytelling that he finds the Lord's deeds far less interesting than their effect on the disciples. The story begins with a setting and exposition[69] as well as a succinct narration of Jesus's disruption of the commerce in the temple area.[70] The Fourth Gospel then stops the action of the scene for a freeze-frame: the author tells us the disciples' inner thoughts; they remember the Psalter's words about zeal for the Lord's house.[71] After three verses of dialogue between Jesus and the Jewish authorities in the Temple,[72] the narrator pauses to comment—"But he was speaking about the temple of his body" (Jn 2:21)—and then tell us how the disciples later remembered the episode: "Therefore, when he was raised from the dead, his disciples remembered that he had said this, and they came to believe the scripture and the word Jesus had spoken" (Jn 2:22). Were the Evangelist's goal to produce suspense in his Gospel, he would have sabotaged it with this clear foreshadowing of how the story of Jesus ends. But the deft construction of the story tells us that the Evangelist had other goals.[73] The story's action terminates abruptly: we hear nothing further of how Jesus and the Jewish authorities resolved their tensions that day in the Temple; such a topic falls outside the Fourth Gospel's interest. Rather, the Evangelist wants to persuade his reader how a true disciple ought to think about Jesus: He fulfills the Old Testament scriptures and is the true Temple, whose raising on the third day after destruction renders the physical one in Jerusalem obsolete.[74] The account concludes with three verses of the narrator's comment, in which he summarizes that many believed in Jesus after they saw the signs He was performing but that this initial faith was untrustworthy because Jesus "had no need for anyone to testify to him concerning humanity for he himself understood what was in humanity" (Jn 2:25, my translation).

The Church reads this pericope[75] on the Third Sunday of Lent in Year B. Because some version of this incident in the Temple occurs in all four Gospels,[76] we can all too easily read the text on a surface level and fail to notice how John's Gospel uniquely chooses to cast the details of what Jesus does. We could rightly draw conclusions about the evils of viewing sacred rites as an occasion for profit or feel ourselves perceiving the enmity that led to the plot on Jesus's life, but we will more fruitfully enter the drama of discipleship—the story the Evangelist is interested in telling—by noticing how John's Gospel constructs the story. It draws us into the story, inviting us through ideological rhetoric to remember this incident with the disciples in the light of the Resurrection and, so, worship the risen Lord and true Temple as would Thomas: "My Lord and my God" (Jn 20:28). Additionally, this story moves us through aesthetic rhetoric to live differently than these early believers in Jesus whose faith was untrustworthy; instead, we want to "remain in" the Lord's love and, thus, bear abundant fruit and truly become His disciples.[77] This careful *lectio*—sensitive to the exegetical tasks of identifying speakers and noting how the inspired storyteller allocates his time between narrated action, direct speech, and narrative commentary[78]—forms a strong foundation for deeper prayer based on all that the Evangelist communicates by his divinely inspired choices.

Hearing the Divine Formator as He Prepares Men to Lead His People

Both passages show how the Lord formed different leaders for his people at different moments in the history of salvation. Solomon had the opportunity to receive kingship as a grace and shepherd his people in the ways of the Lord's law; instead, he chose to consolidate his power by shedding blood, making alliances with foreign powers by marriage, and eventually enriching himself and enabling syncretism in Israel, all with long-term disastrous consequences for God's people. Clergy hold the same awesome and awful power, to lead the Church in holiness or to cause ruin through self-serving scandal. The disciples made a different choice. By remembering the Lord's Resurrection and clinging to the true Temple, they bore witness even to the shedding of their own blood, going where they presumably did not want to go.[79] They certainly committed several missteps and were slow to understand all the Lord told them,[80] but they still chose to remain with the Lord. Prayerful reading of the Sacred Page inspires us to do the same.

NOTES

1. This introductory reflection was deeply inspired by Albert Van-hoye, *Daily Bread of the Word* (Chicago: Liturgy Training Publications, 2019), 510.

2. Benedict XVI, *Verbum Domini* (2010), sec. 76.

3. Francis, *Evangelii Gaudium* (2013), sec. 151.

4. See *Verbum Domini*, sec. 82: "Such attention to the prayerful reading of Scripture must not in any way lead to a dichotomy with regard to the exegetical studies which are a part of formation. The Synod recommended that seminarians be concretely helped to see *the relationship between biblical studies and scriptural prayer*. The study of Scripture ought to lead to an increased awareness of the mystery of divine revelation and foster an attitude of prayerful response to the Lord who speaks. Conversely, an authentic life of prayer cannot fail to nurture in the candidate's heart a desire for greater knowledge of the God who has revealed himself in his word as infinite love. Hence, great care should be taken to ensure that seminarians always cultivate this *reciprocity between study and prayer* in their lives. This end will be served if candidates are introduced to the study of Scripture through methods which favour this integral approach," emphasis in original. See also *Evangelii Gaudium*, sec. 152–53.

5. Konrad Schaefer, "*Lectio Divina* Fosters Growth and Formation," in *Piercing the Clouds: Lectio Divina and Preparation for Ministry*, ed. Kevin Zilverberg and Scott Carl, Catholic Theological Formation Series (St. Paul, MN: Saint Paul Seminary Press, 2021), 57.

6. John Barton, *The Nature of Biblical Criticism* (Louisville: Westminster John Knox, 2007), 114.

7. See, for example, Robert Alter, *The Art of Biblical Narrative* (New York: Basic Books, 1981); Robert Alter, *The Art of Biblical Poetry*, rev. ed. (New York: Basic Books, 2011); Adele Berlin, *Poetics and Interpretation of Biblical Narrative*, Bible and Literature Series (Sheffield: Almond, 1983); Jeannine K. Brown, *The Gospels as Stories: A Narrative Approach to Matthew, Mark, Luke, and John* (Grand Rapids: Baker Academic, 2020); William P. Brown, "Stylistic Analysis II: Narrative," chap. 17 in *A Handbook to Old Testament Exegesis* (Louisville: Westminster John Knox, 2017); Jan P. Fokkelman, *Reading Biblical Narrative: An Introductory Guide* (Louisville: Westminster John Knox, 1999); Robert W. Funk, *The Poetics of Biblical Narrative* (Sonoma, CA: Polebridge, 1988); Jean-Louis Ska, "*Our Fathers Have Told Us*": *Introduction to the Analysis of Hebrew Narratives*, Subsidia biblica 13 (Rome: Editrice Pontificio Istituto Biblico, 2000); Meir Sternberg, *The Poetics of Biblical Narrative: Ideological Literature and the Drama of Reading* (Bloomington, IN: Indiana University Press, 1985).

8. This term "narrative rhetoric" seems to have first appeared in broader literary criticism—which studies all kinds of storytelling—when Seymour Chatman employed it in his *Coming to Terms: Narrative in Fiction and Film* (Ithaca, NY: Cornell University Press, 1990), 203. See also James Phelan, *Narrative as Rhetoric: Technique, Audiences, Ethics, Ideology* (Columbus, OH: Ohio State University Press, 1996) and Michael Kearns, *Rhetorical Narratology* (Lincoln: University of Nebraska Press, 1999). It has increasingly migrated into New Testament scholarship over the last decade: see Paul Danove, "A Method for Analyzing the Semantic and Narrative Rhetoric of Repetition and Their Contributions to Characterization," *Estudios bíblicos* 76 (2018): 55–84. Additionally, Michal Beth Dinkler has contributed several articles focused on the narrative rhetoric of Luke-Acts: see her "New Testament Rhetorical Narratology: An Invitation toward Integration," *Biblical Interpretation* 24 (2016): 203–228; "Building Character on the Road to Emmaus: Lukan Characterization in Contemporary Literary Perspective," *Journal of Biblical Literature* 136, no. 3 (2017): 687–706; "The Politics of Stephen's Storytelling: Narrative Rhetoric and Reflexivity in Acts 7:2–53," *Zeitschrift für die neutestamentliche Wissenschaft und die Kunde den älteren Kirche* 111, no. 1 (2020): 33–64; "The Narrative Rhetoric of Speech and Silence in the Acts of the Apostles," *New Testament Studies* 67, no. 1 (2021): 1–21.

9. For more on these two concepts, see Chatman, *Coming to Terms*, 189.

10. Ibid., 189.

11. Ibid., 203.

12. Although not explicit in 1 Kings, the shepherd metaphor for the work of kings in leading their subjects has Ancient Near Eastern roots that reach as early as the third millennium BC: see Jack W. Vancil, "Sheep, Shepherd," in *Anchor Bible Dictionary* (New York: Doubleday, 1992), 5:1187–88. For biblical examples of this usage, see Psalm 80:2 (of God's rule over his people), 2 Samuel 5:2 (of David's royal rule over Israel), and Ezekiel 34:23 (of a successor of David).

13. See John 1:1, 14.

14. See 2 Samuel 12:24–25.

15. See, for example, Proverbs 1:1, 10:1, 25:1; Ecclesiastes 1:1; Wisdom 7:1–22.

16. See, for example, Sirach 47:19–20; 49:4.

17. The Chronicler famously lionizes Solomon as a paragon of wisdom. Consider, for example, how the Chronicler rehabilitates Solomon's use of forced labor and relationship with Pharaoh's daughter in 2 Chronicles 8:7– 11 in contrast to 1 Kings 5:27–31 (regarding forced laborers from among the Israelites) and 1 Kings 3:1 (regarding Pharaoh's daughter). With regard to the former, although 1 Kings 9:20–22 states that Solomon did not conscript Israelites on at least one occasion, 1 Kings 12:22 (and 2 Chronicles 10:18, for that matter) makes clear that forced labor was one

of the issues that led to the schism under Rehoboam, which would only make sense if Solomon were conscripting Israelites on other occasions as 1 Kings 5:27 indicates. For further support that Solomon did conscript forced laborers from among Israel, see 1 Kings 12:4 and 2 Chronicles 10:4.

18. Because the division into 1 and 2 Kings occurred long after the book was composed, I shall refer to the entire work of 1–2 Kings simply as the Book of Kings. See Choon-Leong Seow, "The First and Second Books of Kings," in *The New Interpreter's Bible* (Nashville: Abingdon, 1999), 3:3–4.

19. Although the tools of narrative rhetoric had not been fully developed by the time of its composition, Jerome T. Walsh's commentary on 1 Kings employs methodology especially well suited to the kind of analysis employed in this study. See Jerome T. Walsh, *1 Kings*, Berit Olam (Collegeville, MN: Liturgical, 1996), xiii–xxi (on methodology) and 3–77 (his treatment of the passages analyzed in this essay).

20. See Sirach 47:12–20.

21. See Sirach 49:4.

22. See 1 Kings 1:8, 32.

23. See 1 Kings 1:34, 39.

24. This language used for describing the ratio of story time (the length of clock time that elapses in the story) to discourse time (the amount of text used to narrate the story) is adapted from vocabulary used to describe film and is described more fully in Seymour Chatman, *Story and Discourse: Narrative Structure in Fiction and Film* (Ithaca, NY: Cornell University Press, 1977), 67–78, and Kearns, *Rhetorical Narratology*, 140–52.

25. Indeed, as Walsh (*1 Kings*, 5) observes, the grammar of the story indicates David's feebleness: he is the subject of no active verbs; all the action is performed upon him.

26. See 1 Kings 1:5–10.

27. See 1 Kings 1:11–14.

28. See 1 Kings 1:15–31.

29. See 1 Kings 1:29–30.

30. See 1 Kings 1:32–37.

31. See 1 Kings 1:38–40.

32. See 1 Kings 1:34, 39, 45.

33. See 1 Kings 1:50. This institution appears obliquely in the covenant code; see Exodus 21:13–14.

34. See 1 Kings 1:53.

35. See 1 Kings 2:1–12.

36. See 1 Kings 2:3–4.

37. See 1 Kings 2:5–9.

38. See 1 Kings 2:13–18.

39. See 1 Kings 2:19.

40. Unless otherwise indicated, all English biblical quotations in this essay come from the New American Bible Revised Edition (NABRE).

41. See 1 Kings 1:3–4.
42. See 1 Kings 1:29–30, 2:24.
43. See 1 Kings 2:25.
44. See 1 Kings 1:50.
45. See 1 Kings 11:1–11.
46. See 1 Kings 2:26–27. This detail finishes the curse on the house of Eli first announced in 1 Samuel 2:30–36, as noted explicitly in 1 Kings 2:27, and likely explains why the priest-prophet Jeremiah—"one of the priests from Anathoth" (Jeremiah 1:1)—takes a hostile stance toward the Temple (see especially Jeremiah 7:1–15 and 26:1–19). For more on this topic, see Marvin A. Sweeney, *The Prophetic Literature*, Interpreting Biblical Texts (Nashville: Abingdon, 2005), 87.
47. See 1 Kings 2:28–35.
48. See 2 Samuel 16:5–13; 19:17–24.
49. See 1 Kings 2:36–46.
50. See Matthew 1:1, 17; Luke 3:31; Romans 1:3.
51. See 2 Kings 25:1-30.
52. See Deuteronomy 7:3 and Joshua 23:12. Here, I defer to the standard theory that the Former Prophets—Joshua, Judges, Samuel, and Kings—broadly follow the theological outlook of Deuteronomy. See Mordechai Cogan, *1 Kings*, Anchor Yale Bible 10 (New Haven: Yale University Press, 2001), 96–100.
53. See especially 1 Samuel 8:19–20 as well as Judges 18:1; 19:1; 21:15. See also Walter Brueggemann, *1 & 2 Kings*, Smyth & Helwys Bible Commentary (Macon, GA: Smyth & Helwys, 2000), 43–45.
54. See Exodus 5:1–5 and 12:31.
55. The Lectionary includes only 1 Kings 2:1–4, 10–12 (David's words to Solomon) at weekday Mass (Thursday of the 4th Week in Ordinary Time during even years), and the Breviary clips in 1 Kings 1:11–35; 2:10–12 (the first part of the succession narrative) on Friday of the Fourteenth Week in Ordinary Time. Never do these liturgical books include Solomon's actions to consolidate his power after taking the throne. This example, thus, demonstrates the value of reading the Bible for its own sake apart from the liturgical cycles. Although the postconciliar Roman Rite has done much to increase familiarity with especially the Old Testament among Catholics, no substitute for contact with the unabridged Sacred Page exists.
56. The Lectionary presents 1 Kings 3:5, 7–12 as the first reading on the Seventeenth Sunday in Ordinary Time in Year A and 1 Kings 3:4–13 on Saturday of the Fourth Week of Ordinary Time during even years.
57. See 1 Kings 3:5–15.
58. See 1 Kings 3:16–28.
59. See 1 Kings 9:20–22, 2 Chronicles 8:7–9.
60. See 1 Kings 12:14-20, 2 Chronicles 10:14–19. For more on the question of whether Solomon conscripted Israelites, see Iain W. Provan,

1 and 2 Kings, New International Bible Commentary: Old Testament Series (Peabody, MA: Hendrickson, 1995), 65, and Brueggemann, *1 & 2 Kings*, 77–81.

61.   Indeed, the Fourth Gospel concentrates this transformation into the post-Resurrection scene on the Sea of Galilee: Peter goes from a unilateral choice to go fishing (21:3a) to an unsuccessful night's fish (21:3b) to a superabundant morning catch with the Risen Lord's aid (21:6) to an invitation to the work of a shepherd (21:15–19).

62.   See John 21:18–19. An important commentary that applied narrative analysis and helped form the foundation for the analysis present here is Francis J. Moloney, *John*, Sacra Pagina 4 (Collegeville, MN: Liturgical, 1998). See especially pages 13–20 on methodology.

63.   The threefold occurrence of "on this day" (Tῇ ἐπαύριον) in John 1:29, 35, and 43 punctuates four days: those narrated in vv. 19–28, vv. 29–34, vv. 35–42, and vv. 43–51, respectively. For more, see Francis J. Moloney, "The First Days of Jesus and the Role of the Disciples: A Study of John 1:19–51," *Australian Biblical Review* 65 (2017): 61–77.

64.   See John 1:40–42.

65.   See John 2:1–10.

66.   See John 2:11.

67.   See John 2:12.

68.   See John 2:13. The second Passover occurs in concert with the feeding miracle and the Bread of Life discourse (see John 6:4), and the third Passover takes place when Jesus endures His Passion in Jerusalem (see John 12:1, 13:1, and 19:14).

69.   See John 2:13–14.

70.   See John 2:15–16.

71.   See John 2:17.

72.   See John 2:18–20.

73.   See Moloney, *John*, 79–80.

74.   See also especially Jesus's words to the woman at the well about Temple worship in John 4:21–24. See also Andrew T. Lincoln, *The Gospel according to Saint John*, Black's New Testament Commentaries (London: Continuum, 2005), 138–41.

75.   See John 2:13–25.

76.   See Matthew 21:12–13, Mark 11:15–19, and Luke 19:45–46.

77.   See John 15:7–10.

78.   For more on how to analyze narratives with attention to these features, see Kearns, *Rhetorical Narratology*, 99–113.

79.   See John 21:18–19.

80.   See, for example, John 4:32, 13:7, 14:5, and 16:8.

LECTIO DIVINA AT THE HEART OF PRIESTLY FORMATION: FORMING THE HEARTS OF PROPHETS FOR THE KINGDOM

XIMENA DEBROECK

The *Ratio Fundamentalis Institutionis Sacerdotalis* of 1970 was amended in 1985 to reflect the 1983 Code of Canon Law. In 2016, some three decades later, the Congregation for the Clergy, with the approval of Pope Francis, promulgated a new document, "The Gift of the Priestly Vocation: *Ratio Fundamentalis Institutionis Sacerdotalis.*"[1] The new *Ratio* stands in continuity with other documents that address priestly formation, and yet it offers a nuanced perspective about the process of formation. The new *Ratio* builds on the paradigm of the four dimensions of formation: human, spiritual, intellectual, and pastoral, articulated in *Pastores Dabo Vobis;* and it continues with the language of "journey," used in *Pastores Dabo Vobis* as vocational journey.[2] With nuanced language, the *Ratio Fundamentalis* indicates that the journey is characterized by four elements: (1) one singular journey, (2) an integrated process, (3) grounded in community, and (4) missionary in spirit.[3] In this document, as well as in previous documents on priestly formation, the centrality of God's Word, particularly the practice of *lectio divina*, along the formative journey is vital.[4]

In this essay, I will focus on the image of *journey* and offer three points of reflection for seminary formators to ponder. First, we will enter into our own moment of *lectio*, as we meditate on the call of three prophets and encounter the *journey of a prophet as a Teacher of the Word*. Second, we will consider creative ways to incorporate *lectio* in all aspects of priestly formation and, thus, imagine a *journey across the formation stages and dimensions*. Lastly, we will consider the centrality of God's Word in the four unique elements of the new *Ratio*, and so approach the *Ratio Fundamentalis as a guided journey*.

Teacher of the Word—The Journey of a Prophet

"Now indeed I know that you are a man of God, and it is truly the word of the Lord that you speak." 1 Kgs 17:24

Priestly identity is the core of priestly formation; it constitutes the basis and purpose of the formational journey. This calling received at baptism necessarily precedes the calling to ministerial priesthood.[5] Therefore, the priestly identity must be rooted in the baptismal identity. In baptism, the man was consecrated as priest, prophet, and king.[6] These three roles will be lived out in a unique way in the ministerial priesthood, and the Word of God is central to all three. In this regard, the *Ratio Fundamentalis* states,

> As a member of the holy People of God, the priest is called to cultivate his missionary zeal, exercising his pastoral responsibility with humility as an authoritative leader, teacher of the Word and minister of the sacraments,[7] practicing his spiritual fatherhood fruitfully.[8]

Considering the many responsibilities of the priest, the Church teaches that the primary duty of the priest is to preach the Word, which is indeed needed for the celebration of all sacraments.[9] Given the centrality of God's Word in priestly formation, this essay begins by focusing on the priest as *Teacher of the Word*. To this end, I suggest a reflection on three biblical prophets.

The role of the prophet is commonly defined as mediator between God and the people, as an intercessor, as someone who anoints a king (at God's bidding), as someone who condemns or authorizes war (at God's command)—in summary, as the Lord's messenger. Yet, with all these roles, often the prophet's fundamental calling is overlooked. Indeed, a prophet is a messenger; however, this role needs to be properly understood in the context of the prophetic call. First and foremost, a prophet is called to remind the people of the covenant, which begins with listening to God's Word and obeying it, as the great *Shema* prayer[10] reminds us. Therefore, all that a prophet does flows out of this call. A prophet warns the people and speaks oracles of denunciation to those who have abandoned the covenant. A prophet also consoles the people and delivers prophecies of blessing and hope to those who have stayed faithful to the covenant, and/or who repent and return to the covenantal relationship.

A prophet is able to live his calling—his vocation—only as he grows in intimacy with God's Word. Therefore, daily encounters with and meditation of the Word of God are vital for the prophetic ministry of a priest.[11] And now, I invite us to enter into our own moment of *lectio* as we meditate on the call of three prophets and enter into the *journey of a prophet*, through encounters that Isaiah, Jeremiah, and Ezekiel had with the Word.

Let us accompany Isaiah; let us journey to a time of great suffering for God's people, when the Lord speaks about a servant whom God has chosen for a mission. We can imagine hearing the prophet telling us,

> The Lord God has given me a well-trained tongue, That I might know how to answer the weary a word that will waken them. Morning after morning he wakens my ear to hear as disciples do; The Lord God opened my ear; I did not refuse, did not turn away. (Is 50:4–5)

The Lord opened Isaiah's ear, and he did not turn away; he listened, and God gave him the means to communicate words of consolation.

Now we will journey with Jeremiah as he tells us about his encounter with God's Word:

> The word of the Lord came to me:
> Before I formed you in the womb I knew you,
> before you were born I dedicated you,
> a prophet to the nations I appointed you.
> "Ah, Lord God!" I said,
> "I do not know how to speak. I am too young!"
> But the Lord answered me,
> Do not say, "I am too young."
> To whomever I send you, you shall go;
> whatever I command you, you shall speak.
> Do not be afraid of them,
> for I am with you to deliver you—oracle of the Lord.
> Then the Lord extended his hand and touched my mouth,
> saying to me, See, I place my words in your mouth!
> (Jer 1:4–9)

Following a classical pattern of the prophetic call, Jeremiah struggles to understand and accept the call. He voices his concerns, indicating that because of his youth, he is unable to speak as a messenger of the Lord. Yet, the Lord assures him, "See, I place my words in your mouth!" (Jer 1:9)

Next, we journey to ancient Babylon, and we can imagine sitting by the shore of the River Chebar and with Ezekiel, can receive these words:

> You must speak my words to them, whether they hear or resist, because they are rebellious. But you, son of man, hear me when I speak to you and do not rebel like this rebellious house. Open your mouth and eat what I am giving you. (Ez 2:7–8)

> He said to me: Son of man, eat what you find here: eat this scroll, then go, speak to the house of Israel. So I opened my mouth, *and he gave me the scroll to eat* [emphasis added]. Son of man, he said to me, feed your stomach and fill your belly with this scroll I am giving you. I ate it, and it was as sweet as honey in my mouth. Then he said to me, Son of man, go now to the house of Israel, and speak my words to them. (Ez 3:1–4)

Ezekiel receives the call to announce God's Word to rebellious people. If that is not a daunting task . . . The setting is different today, and yet, much is the same. Humanity continues to be rebellious, and God's Word still needs to be announced.

Each of these three prophets had a unique encounter with God's Word; each of them received a unique call within the general prophetic call as a teacher of God's Word and love. Isaiah's ears were opened, and his tongue was equipped to articulate the words he needed to speak. Jeremiah did not know how to speak, and the Lord placed the Divine Word in his mouth; Jeremiah then spoke God's words. Ezekiel was tasked with speaking God's Word to an audience not ready to hear it, and the only way he was able to carry out the mission was after consuming the Word.

A Journey across the Formation Stages and Dimensions

"Consecrate them in the truth. Your word is truth." Jn 17:17

In this next section, I will share thoughts about a journey with God's Word across the formation dimensions and stages, as articulated by the *Ratio Fundamentalis.*

Human formation being the foundation of all priestly formation[12] aims at the daunting task of accompanying men in a process of self-discovery and self-awareness. As the seminarian acknowledges his gifts, he grows in gratitude to God. At the same time, the seminarian is able to name areas of weakness in character and in virtue, areas of woundedness that need healing, and learned patterns of unhealthy coping mechanisms. The formation sessions can become monotonous as goal after goal is discussed, and outcomes are evaluated. I suggest incorporating *lectio* in this area. According to the needs of the seminarian, the formator could begin the formation session with a time of *lectio*, which can help illumine the path ahead in human formation.

Spiritual formation aims at guiding the journey to communion with God as the man grows in friendship with Jesus and docility to the Holy Spirit.[13] This is probably the dimension of formation that most naturally connects with time spent meditating with God's Word.[14] During the scheduled spiritual direction meetings and the annual retreats, seminarians are most likely to practice *lectio*. The seminarian needs to be mindful that, "Before it [the Word of God] is ever preached, the Word must be welcomed in the depth of the heart."[15] This is possible through regular time spent in *lectio*.

Intellectual formation targets giving the seminarian a solid academic foundation to allow him "to proclaim the Gospel message to the people of our own day in a way that is credible and can be understood. It seeks to enable them to enter into fruitful dialogue with the contemporary world. . . . "[16] Since Scripture is the soul of theology,[17] Scripture should be woven across the entire curriculum. Indeed, professors of all seminary courses should be mindful of the words of Leo XIII, "Most desirable is it, and most essential, that the whole teaching of Theology should be pervaded and animated by the use of the divine Word of God."[18] Having Scripture as a foundation of all courses is essential; however, more should be done to integrate God's sacred Word with the study of various academic courses. Regular periods of lectio can be included in every course. It might seem as though it could distract the "flow" of the course that we might have imagined or anticipated. But what could be more fruitful than allowing God's Word to speak to the seminarian directly during a given lecture? When teaching Christology, instead of speaking about the Christological hymns of Philippians 2 and Colossians 1, some time devoted to lectio can be part of that day's lecture. Or, perhaps, during a course on Baptism and Confirmation, time devoted to lectio on Ezekiel 36:25–32, John 4, John 9, and John 11 can be a blessed opportunity of encounter. As part of a Canon Law course, in the context of presenting canon 773, the seminarians could be offered time for lectio on Malachi 2:7–9.

Pastoral formation aims at guiding the seminarian toward an integration of the other dimensions. The seminarian prepares to serve God's people with a heart molded after the Good Shepherd. Seminaries are meticulous in coordinating placement for Pastoral Field Education. In the formators' collaboration with the field supervisors, the seminarian is assisted in this dimension. An integral aspect of pastoral formation is the practice of theological reflection,[19] which offers the seminarian the opportunity to reflect on a pastoral experience in the light of Scripture and Church teaching.[20] Although this is a common practice in the course of pastoral formation, I suggest we can integrate *lectio* in other ways in pastoral formation. Seminarians should be encouraged to include *lectio* as part of their ministry in the different placements. During a placement in faith formation, they can introduce young children and adolescents to *lectio*. When visiting the sick and homebound, the seminarian can include *lectio* in his pastoral visit. As the seminarian is preparing a couple for marriage or presenting a session for RCIA, he can begin with *lectio* or include a time of *lectio* at some point during the presentation. The possibilities are truly endless and quite fruitful.

Each of the new stages of formation, presented in the *Ratio Fundamentalis*, is constituted by the four dimensions of formation. As mentioned above, the integration of *lectio* across the dimensions is not only possible, but it should also be normative.

- In the *propaudeutic stage*, as the seminarian begins an intentional journey of the interior life, "familiarity with the Word of God, which is to be considered the soul and guide for the journey"[21] is essential.

- During the *discipleship stage*, the seminarian is rooted in the *sequela Christi*; and therefore, it is fundamental to practice the "listening to His Word [God's Word], keeping it in his heart and putting it into practice."[22]

- In the *configuration stage*, as his studies continue, an intentional ongoing practice of *lectio* will prepare the seminarian for future service as a lector and acolyte. "Lectorate challenges the seminarian to allow himself to be transformed by the Word of God, the object of his prayer and study. The conferral of the ministry of acolyte implies a deeper participation in the mystery of Christ, who gives Himself and is present in the Eucharist, in the assembly, and in His brothers and sisters."[23] The closer the seminarian is to the Word inspired, the closer the configuration to the Word Incarnate.

- As the time in seminary ends, and the *vocational synthesis stage* begins, the ongoing formation should be accompanied by the practice of *lectio*. During fraternal meetings, there is the possibility of reading God's Word together.[24] Living in community, in a rectory or religious house, is a setting not simply to "share a living space," but also to truly practice a common life of prayer and meditation on God's Word.[25]

Ratio Fundamentalis as a Guided Journey

"Your word is a lamp for my feet, a light for my path." Ps 119:105

The journey of formation invites the seminarian to transformation, one that demands "daily contact with the Word of God."[26] The present *Ratio* describes the journey of priestly formation as having four defining elements: (1) one singular journey, (2) an integrated process, (3) grounded in community, and (4) missionary in spirit.[27]

Singular Journey Process—"a singular 'journey is one of dis-cipleship', which begins at Baptism, [and] is perfected through the other sacraments of Christian initiation."[28] This journey deepens in commitment throughout life and must continue after ordination. At every step of the way, the seminarian is invited and urged to meditate on God's Word day and night. Every Sunday of week 1, as the seminarian prays the Office of Readings, he will be reminded to ponder God's law [given by His Word] day and night (Ps 1); or on Monday of week 3, as he prays daytime prayer, he will pray "Your word, Lord, stands forever; it is firm as the heavens" (Ps 119:89); and every Sunday for Evening Prayer I of week 2, as well as for daytime prayer of Wednesday of week 3, he will meditate on "Your word is a lamp for my feet, a light for my path" (Ps 119:105).

Integrated Process—the four dimensions are not isolated paths, rather they inform and influence each other. When the paths are understood as an integral unit, one can easily appreciate that the four dimensions together provide a seamless feedback path. The new *Ratio* clearly articulates that "the entire journey of formation must never be reduced to a single aspect to the detriment of others, but it must always be an integrated journey of the disciple called to priesthood."[29] This integration has already been expressed in previous documents.[30] The cur-rent *Ratio Fundamentalis* continues to emphasize this charac-teristic of the formation process.

Community Process—the community is the place of nour-ishment of the vocation and the place where the seminarian will live out his consecrated service and the environment of all else between these two. "Such a vocation is discovered and accepted within a community. It is formed in the Seminary, in the context of an educating community, comprised of various members of the People of God. This community leads the seminarian through ordination, to become part of the 'family' of the presbyterate, at the service of a particular community."[31] The role of the community is foundational. The community should live out its own prophetic vocation and guide the seminarian continuously along the path of God's Word. We can say that "it takes a village" to form a seminarian.

Missionary Process—this aspect of the journey returns our thoughts to the baptismal call, when the seeds of missionary discipleship were planted in the soul of the seminarian. " . . . Seminaries should form missionary disciples who are 'in love' with the Master, shepherds 'with the smell of the sheep', who live in their midst to bring the mercy of God to them."[32] Reading the accounts of the earliest Christian communities, we can appreciate the missionary impulse of God's Word:

> Perusing the Acts of the Apostles, one realises [*sic*] the transformative effect of the Word of God, that interior power that brings about the conversion of hearts. The Word is the food that nourishes the Lord's disciples and makes them witnesses to the Gospel in the various circumstances of life. The Scriptures contain a prophetic impetus that makes them into a living force. It is necessary to provide instruction on how to listen and mediate on the Word of God through a variety of different approaches to proclamation, adopting clear and comprehensible means of communication that announce the Lord Jesus according to the ever new witness of the kerygma.[33]

In summary, the image of journey has provided us a way to enter into this reflection. Seminary formation can be appreciated through the journey of a prophet as a teacher of the Word, who enters a journey through stages and dimensions, with the Word of the Lord and the practice of *lectio divina*, as a light on the path of the guided journey proposed by the new *Ratio*.

We are reminded that

- God opens the ears of the prophet; the prophet does not turn away.

- God puts His Words in the prophet's mouth; the prophet accepts the Word and is able to preach and teach.

- God asks the prophet to fill his appetite with His Word; the prophet consumes the Word and can then communicate it to the people.

It all begins with the divine initiative, but a response to the gift is required. The prophets cooperate by not turning away, accepting the Word, and consuming the Word. What would this look like for men in priestly formation? God has begun the work. Our role as formators, with the intentional practice of *lectio divina*, is to guide and cultivate dispositions that can allow the men to respond to the prophetic call.

"Let the word of Christ dwell in you richly, as in all wisdom you teach and admonish one another, singing psalms, hymns, and spiritual songs with gratitude in your hearts to God." (Col 3:16)

NOTES

1. Congregation for the Clergy, *Ratio Fundamentalis Institutionis Sacerdotalis* (2016).
2. John Paul II, *Pastores Dabo Vobis* (1992), sec. 9, 43, 61, 64.
3. *Ratio Fundamentalis*, Introduction, sec. 3.
4. Ibid., sec. 103. Refer also to Paul VI, *Optatam Totius* (1965), sec. 8: "They should be taught to seek Christ in the faithful meditation on God's Word, in the active participation in the sacred mysteries of the Church, especially in the Eucharist and in the divine office, in the bishop who sends them and in the people to whom they are sent, especially the poor, the children, the sick, the sinners and the unbelievers." See John Paul II, *Pastores Dabo Vobis* (1992), sec. 47: "An essential element of spiritual formation is the prayerful and meditated reading of the word of God (*lectio divina*), a humble and loving listening of him who speaks. It is in fact by the light and with the strength of the word of God that one's own vocation can be discovered and understood, loved and followed, and one's own mission carried out. So true is this that the person's entire existence finds its unifying and radical meaning in being the terminus of God's word which calls man and the beginning of man's word which answers God. Familiarity with the word of God will make conversion easy, not only in the sense of detaching us from evil so as to adhere to the good, but also in the sense of nourishing our heart with the thoughts of God, so that the faith (as a response to the word) becomes our new basis for judging and evaluating persons and things, events and problems"; see also Benedict XVI, *Verbum Domini* (2010), sec. 82, 86, 87; additionally, see Francis, *Evangelii Gaudium* (2013), sec. 152. Pope Francis here addresses the importance of *lectio divina* in preparation for preaching.
5. Paul VI, *Lumen Gentium* (1964), sec. 10–11.
6. See Order of Baptism, explanatory rites, the anointing after baptism: "He now anoints you with the Chrism of salvation, so that you may remain members of Christ, Priest, Prophet and King."
7. Congregation for the Clergy, *The Priest and the Third Christian Millennium, Teacher of the Word, Minister of the Sacraments and Leader of the Community* (1999).
8. *Ratio Fundamentalis*, chapter III, sec. 33.
9. Paul VI, *Presbyterorum Ordinis* (1965), sec. 4: "In the Christian community, especially among those who seem to understand and believe little of what they practice, the preaching of the word is needed for the very ministering of the sacraments. They are precisely sacraments of faith, a faith which is born of and nourished by the word." See also *Code of Canon Law*, sec. 762.

10.   See Deuteronomy 6:4–7: "Hear, O Israel! The Lord is our God, the Lord alone! Therefore, you shall love the Lord, your God, with your whole heart, and with your whole being, and with your whole strength. Take to heart these words which I command you today. Keep repeating them to your children."

11.   *Pastores Dabo Vobis*, sec. 47: "A loving knowledge of the word of God and a prayerful familiarity with it are specifically important for the *prophetic ministry of the priest*. They are a fundamental condition for such a ministry to be carried out suitably, especially if we bear in mind the 'new evangelization' which the Church today is called to undertake. The Council tells us: 'All clerics, particularly priests of Christ and others who, as deacons or catechists, are officially engaged in the ministry of the word, should immerse themselves in the Scriptures by constant sacred reading and diligent study. For it must not happen that anyone becomes "an empty preacher of the word of God to others, not being a hearer of the word of God in his own heart" (St. Augustine, Sermon 179, 1: PL 8:966),'" emphasis added.

12.   Ibid., 43.

13.   *Presbyterorum Ordinis*, sec. 12.

14.   *Ratio Fundamentalis*, chapter V, sec. 102.

15.   Ibid., sec.103.

16.   Ibid., sec. 116.

17.   Ibid., sec. 166, See Paul VI, *Dei Verbum* (1965), sec. 24; see also Leo XIII, *Providentissimus Deus* (1893), sec. 16.

18.   Ibid.

19.   *Pastores Dabo Vobis*, sec. 57; see also United States Conference of Catholic Bishops (USCCB), Program of Priestly Formation, 6th ed. (Washington DC: USCCB, 2022), sec. 345.

20.   *Program of Priestly Formation*, sec. 320, 326.

21.   *Ratio Fundamentalis*, chapter IV, sec. 59.

22.   Ibid., chapter IV, sec. 62.

23.   Ibid., sec.72.

24.   Ibid., sec. 88a.

25.   Ibid., sec. 88e.

26.   Ibid., chapter III, sec. 43.

27.   Ibid., Introduction, sec. 3.

28.   Ibid.

29.   Ibid.

30.   *Ratio Fundamentalis* (1985) Intro, no. 1 and chapter 12, no. 79; See also *Pastores Dabo Vobis* sec. 51, 71.

31.   *Ratio Fundamentalis* (2016), Introduction, sec. 3.

32.   Ibid.

33.   Congregation for the Clergy, *The Pastoral Conversion of the Parish Community in the Service of the Evangelising Mission of the Church* (2020), sec. 21.

THE PRACTICE OF LECTIO DIVINA
AND PRIESTLY FORMATION

MARK O'KEEFE, O.S.B.

A priest is a man of Christ, a man of the Church, and, therefore, a man of the Word of God. The same could be said of every baptized Christian—united with Christ and destined for union with Him by baptism, incorporated into the life of the Body of Christ, and needing regular encounter with the Word to be fed and formed in the life of Christ. But by ordination, the priest is uniquely configured to Christ in order to live and minister in His person (*in persona Christi*), and the contributors to this volume have reminded us that there cannot be a fully authentic priestly life and ministry—or priestly formation—without a special commitment to becoming always more deeply immersed in God's Word. The priest is fed, formed, and transformed precisely as a priest in an ongoing way through communion with Christ who is made present in the Scriptures. As William Wright notes, when we speak of the Word of God, we are speaking of a "who" more than a "what." The possibility of transformation—rather than simply increased knowledge—is its fruit.

79

Lectio divina, as we have been reminded in these pages, is a time-honored and even cherished path to a deeper reading of the Bible. Several of our contributors have emphasized that its fruitful practice can be enhanced by a background in and the practice of sound contemporary biblical interpretation. Seminarians are uniquely blessed to have the opportunity to be formed in graduate level scriptural studies by which they can enter more deeply into the rich layers of meaning in every divinely inspired text. They are more aware of sound resources to help them in this task. Stephen Fahrig points out that the more that one knows about the text, the more avenues that the Holy Spirit has available to reveal a living word for the priest and the people.

Ancient Christian authors taught that beyond the literal meaning of the biblical text, there are more profound levels that are waiting to be discovered—and ultimately, a spiritual or mystical message embedded in the text. Here, the word "mystical" refers to the something "hidden" or "secret" in the sense that there is a meaning that can only be discovered with eyes of faith. By this, we do not mean that God has intentionally hidden a message as a static, general, conceptual gem waiting to be discovered. Rather, the living Christ who is present in the written and proclaimed Word of God reveals Himself anew and speaks a particular word to a particular person and community in each new reading of the text—for those who approach it with a mature faith, in a spirit of prayer, and with a humility that is willing to be challenged and ready to be obedient. The discovery of this mystical meaning is enhanced by familiarity with and practice in contemporary biblical interpretation.

Llane Briese, in particular, has reminded us that seminarians need guidance to see the connection between what they are studying in their Scripture classes and their personal prayer. The monks who first taught the practice of *lectio* believed that the Bible is the foundation of any authentic Christian life. At the same time, it is a life of prayer that makes possible a deep encounter with Christ in the biblical text. The theology taught in medieval monastic institutions was based on the presupposition that the life of faith and prayer feeds the study of theology while theology, in turn, nurtures faith and communion with God. This is a truth that must be conveyed throughout seminary formation. Ximena DeBroeck rightly challenges us to see that formation in *lectio* is broader than the academic and not restricted to a particular stage of formation.

The Problem of Reading in Our Culture

Lectio divina is not simply another name for spiritual reading understood in the broad sense of reading books on spiritual topics—an encounter that might be done with deep attention or, on the other hand, quite casually. Through *lectio divina*, one seeks a deeper encounter with Christ, especially in the Bible. As a practice, it involves a slow, meditative reading with time and inner space for silence and listening. A person of prayer profitably engages in it with preparation but without preconceived notions of what particular texts mean. It does not have an immediate practical purpose or result.

Trends in our culture and the reality of academic formation in the seminary can mitigate against the kind of reading required in *lectio*. A 2021 Gallup poll reveals that the popularity of reading in our culture is on a steady decline.[1] Twenty years earlier, a study conducted for the National Endowment

for the Arts had concluded that the percentage of adults reading literature had dropped dramatically in the previous twenty
years, paralleling a decline in general book reading and correlated with the increased use of electronic media, the internet,
and video games. Further, the rate of decline is accelerating
and is more pronounced among men than women.[2] In short,
contemporary seminarians come out of a culture in which
reading, beyond for work or some other practical purpose,
is declining—replaced in many cases by the brief and direct
information available from Tweets and a quick Google search.
This reality is compounded by the fact that many seminarians
come without academic backgrounds in the liberal arts, that is,
without practice in reading literature and appreciating music
and the arts, all of which develop the imagination and promote
a comfort with engaging with and discovering meaning in sym-
bols, images, and metaphors.

Formation in *lectio divina* requires attending to the current
state of reading in the culture from which seminarians come.
Scripture classes introduce seminarians to a sense of the Bible
as literature, including its various genres and images. More
broadly, the development of the propaedeutic year in seminary
formation may be an opportunity to introduce the reading of
good literature, a deeper understanding of film, and the appreciation of art (including good liturgical art, ancient and contemporary). Extracurricular seminary reading groups throughout seminary formation can invite the reading and informal
discussion of Catholic literature and important Catholic writers including Hispanic and African-American. The reading of
novels or short stories can be incorporated into various classes
with grading, if necessary, based on participation rather than

an exam or a paper. Such practices can encourage reading that does not have an immediate practical purpose and that requires a deeper engagement with texts, further enriched by dialogue with others.

Academic formation in the seminary can be rigorous and demanding. The seminarians are required to do a great deal of reading for papers and exams. This necessary reality can make it more difficult for the seminarian to develop the kind of meditative reading that *lectio divina* requires. Even their reading in Scripture classes can encourage an attitude in reading that seeks a practical purpose. The contributors to this volume have rightly highlighted the central place of preaching in the life and ministry of a priest. The practice of *lectio divina* brings the deeper reading and encounter with the Word that serves the preaching ministry. At the same time, the too-immediate connection of *lectio* with preaching—which is a principal preoccupation of seminarians—can too easily reduce *lectio* to a practical, almost utilitarian tool narrowly oriented to preparing good homilies. While using the lectionary readings for the current year can be a deeply enriching experience, seminarians can benefit from *lectio* with biblical texts that will not appear in the current year. *Lectio* promotes a deeper life of prayer and communion with the Incarnate Word of God and, thereby, it can bring the seminarian and priest into a deeper conformity to Christ. It is as such more foundational formation that serves all of the practical aspects of priestly ministry.

Preparation for the Practice

Classically, as we have been reminded, *lectio divina* involves four basic moments or steps: *lectio, meditatio, oratio,* and *contemplatio* (reading, meditation, prayer, and contemplation).

Furthermore, our authors have offered us the important reminder that the prayer of *lectio* is not complete without the subsequent *actio* (action). All authentic prayer bears fruit in good action. But in order to form the practice of *lectio* in the lives of seminarians, descriptions and explanations are necessary but not sufficient. *Lectio* is a prayer practice that requires examples, experience, practice, and mentoring.

In these pages, we have seen how critical biblical study can help to bring important formation and tools for the initial step of *lectio*—reading the text with a preparation to encounter its deeper meaning. Our authors have offered insightful and rich examples of how this can work. But what does "meditation" mean in this context? The word, in common parlance, can mean either an active pondering or it can be the equivalent of the wordless prayer that is traditionally called contemplation. Spiritual formation programs, spirituality classes, and spiritual directors can introduce seminarians to the various forms of meditation that have been practiced in the Catholic tradition—whether, for example, imagining oneself within the action of the text or learning to ask questions of it. Without such practical guidance, *meditatio* might remain a nebulous concept and, therefore, be difficult to put into practice.

In like manner, the word "contemplation" can have various meanings, and formators cannot assume that seminarians will intuitively grasp what it means in the context of *lectio*. Again, spiritual formation programs, spirituality classes, and spiritual directors can introduce seminarians to how contemplation has been understood in the Catholic tradition. Of particular help are forms of "acquired" contemplation, as distinct from the classic meaning of "infused" contemplation as the wordless prayer that only comes as a gift from God. The literature of contemporary contemplative practice,[3] often based on the Jesus Prayer of the Eastern Church or on the practice counselled by medieval classic *The Cloud of Unknowing*, can give seminarians a sense of what the *contemplatio* moment of *lectio* might look like. A common practice in *lectio*, for example, is the silent repetition of a word or a phrase that drew the reader's attention in the initial reading of the text. The repetition is at least a tool to draw back one's wandering attention when distractions almost inevitably arise, but the goal and the hope is to arrive at a time of quiet resting and attentiveness to the silent presence of God.

Perhaps more basic and urgent for the promotion of *lectio* is conveying the message that contemplation is not something foreign to any Christian spirituality. An introduction to contemporary discussions of "ordinary mysticism" or "the mysticism of everyday" might help to widen the seminarians' view of how every Christian life can be contemplative in spirit and open to the mystical presence of God in the ordinary. It is true that diocesan priests are not contemplative monks. Their lives can be busy and hectic, but the recognition that their vocation is not, strictly speaking, contemplative should not mean that their prayer should not have some regular experience of contemplative quiet. Today's seminarians and young priests are drawn to spending time in the presence of the Blessed Sacrament. Perhaps they are in less need of repeated challenges, as they progress in prayer, to spend time in quiet prayer (perhaps aided by the contemporary practices mentioned above); but they must be encouraged not to fill their holy hours with only the Liturgy of the Hours or spiritual reading. Formation for *lectio divina* requires that seminarians be disabused of the idea that contemplation—at least as the culmination of the practice of *lectio* in the time regularly committed to it—is foreign to the busy lives of parish priests. The temptation to short-circuit prayer for the sake of pastoral tasks (that could be delayed or done by others) will come soon enough.

Starting a Practice

Early in seminary formation, it may be useful to involve the seminarians in a guided group practice of *lectio* in order to make them comfortable with it and to lay the groundwork for their individual practice. Here is one possible format: Small groups, guided by a formator or by seminarians chosen from the later years of formation, gather. The session opens with a prayer. The *lectio*: the chosen text is then read aloud slowly. After a few minutes of silence, the seminarians are invited to simply say aloud a word or phrase that drew their attention. The *meditatio*: the text is read again. After a few minutes of silence, the participants are invited to share a brief thought on what God might be saying in the Word. The *oratio*: the text is read again, and the seminarians are invited to offer a brief spontaneous prayer of response. The *contemplatio*: all are invited to remain in silence, perhaps silently repeating the word or phrase that struck them from the text or from the thoughts and prayers offered by others. The session concludes with a prayer lead by the group leader. In individual practice, the use of commentaries can enhance the reading and meditation; but here, it is probably best to avoid the temptation for the seminarians to unconsciously prepare a meditation and prayer in advance of the exercise as it unfolds in the group, guided in the moment by the Holy Spirit.

Lectio Divina and the Formation of a Priestly Identity

The spirituality of the priest must be distinctively Christocentric—Christ in His Word, Christ in the Eucharist and other sacraments, Christ present and active in the priest's daily ministry, Christ encountered and served in the people in the good and the bad. This truth is preeminently clear in the Eucharist, when the priest stands in the place of Christ, acting in the person of Christ. At the consecration, when the priest repeats the words of Jesus—"This is my Body. . . . This is my Blood"—the priest identifies himself with Christ and makes those words an expression of his own renewed commitment to lay down his life for the flock. As Saint John Paul II taught, this is the fundamental meaning of pastoral charity—the distinctive virtue for priests. The True Shepherd lays down His life for the flock. This identity and commitment is lived out in the daily, generous, self-forgetful, often very ordinary ministry of the priest.

In the Eucharistic Liturgy, the proclamation and breaking open of God's Word is the doorway that leads to the celebration of Eucharist and, beyond it, to the generous living of the Christian life. So too for the priest, his daily deep encounter with the Word through the practice of *lectio divina* can be a doorway to his presiding at and offering of the Eucharist and, beyond it, to his daily generous ministry firmly grounded in the virtue of pastoral charity.

The priest is a man of the Word because he is a Christian, like his sisters and brothers, who encounters Christ alive and present in the Scriptures. He is a man of the Word because he is distinctively called to serve as a minister of that Word, to break it open for the lives of the people or to allow it to break open the lives of the people to the always present Christ in His divine

Spirit. This means that the priest must truly immerse himself in the Word of God. For preaching, he must give real priority to study and prayer over the Scriptures and their meaning for *this* people at *this* time. He cannot allow himself to fall into the habit of preparing a homily while sitting in the reconciliation room late on a Saturday afternoon without time for a real examination and prayerful reflection of the text.

But the immersion of the priest in God's Word is more than a matter of preparing good homilies. The priest studies and engages the Scriptures because it is there that he encounters Christ and His example and message, in both the New and the Old Testaments. Through the regular practice of *lectio* over biblical texts—through attentive reading, prayerful meditation, a response in prayer from the heart, and quiet resting with the Word—the priest not only learns about Christ and His message, he communes with Him. The priest enters into communion with the mystical—hidden, secret, available only to the eyes of faith—presence of Christ. He forms a deeper bond with Christ and a deeper engagement of his own identity as one who acts in the very person of Christ. Ancient Christian authors spoke of a moral meaning beyond the literal meaning of the text. By reading about and reflecting on the life and example of Jesus in the Gospels, the priest can draw lessons on how he should live and act. But *lectio divina* leads beyond the literal and the moral to the mystical or spiritual meaning of the Word. It thereby can yield a knowledge that is not only intellectual but also a kind of loving and more immediate knowledge of Christ—an engagement, not only of one's mind but also of the heart. *Lectio divina* seeks, not only knowledge *about* Christ, but knowledge *of* Christ to Whom the priest is distinctively configured.

Conclusion

The classic four-step practice of *lectio divina* taught first by a medieval Carthusian is an invaluable and time-honored path for deep engagement with the Word of God. But what is important is not a method or the care in following certain steps. In every authentic form of Christian prayer, it is the Spirit who must lead and teach. What is essential for the seminarian and for the priest is not how he engages the Word, but rather that he does so. Seminarians are blessed to have the opportunity to study Scripture, and they should do so with a spirit of gratitude and with a hunger to learn.

Saint Thomas Aquinas wrote about the virtue of *studiositas* which is the habitual disposition to earnestly seek knowledge that is good, worthy, and important. It is opposed by the vice of *curiositas* which we might call "idle curiosity"—evident in our day in endless Google searches, perusing of Twitter feeds, and viewing of twenty-four-hour news networks. Seminarians—privileged as Christians to study the Bible and blessed to be called to be its ordained ministers—should be encouraged to engage their study of the Bible (together with the rest of their academic formation) with a solid *studiositas*. At the same time, even as they approach the Scriptures with a genuine intellectual curiosity and rigor, they must do so as men of faith and prayer. Prayer yields insights that study alone cannot—even as study feeds and supports a life of prayer. More deeply still, a prayerful engagement with God's Word in *lectio divina*—a spirit of prayerfulness—can bring encounter and even communion with Christ to whom the priest is distinctively configured.

NOTES

1. https://news.gallup.com/poll/388541/americans-reading-fewer-books-past.aspx (accessed December 1, 2022).

2. https://www.arts.gov/sites/default/files/RaRExec.pdf (accessed December 1, 2022).

3. See, for example: Martin Laird, *Into the Silent Land: A Guide to the Christian Practice of Contemplation* (New York: Oxford University Press, 2006).